DEATH AND THE ADOLESCENT

A Resource Handbook for Bereavement Support Groups in Schools

Grant Baxter and Wendy Stuart

UNIVERSITY OF TORONTO PRESS
Toronto Buffalo London

© University of Toronto Press Incorporated 1999
Toronto Buffalo London
Printed in Canada

ISBN 0-8020-0820-8 (cloth)
ISBN 0-8020-7812-5 (paper)

Printed on acid-free paper

Canadian Cataloguing in Publication Data

Baxter, Grant
   Death and the adolescent : a resource handbook for bereavement
   support groups in schools

   Includes bibliographical references.
   ISBN 0-8020-0820-8 (bound)   ISBN 0-8020-7812-5 (pbk.)

   1. Student assistance programs.   2. Bereavement in adolescence.
   3. Teenagers and death.   I. Stuart, Wendy.   II. Title.

BF724.3.D43B393 1999   373.14'6   C98-931709-9

The two articles in Appendix 3 are reprinted with permission of The
Toronto Star Syndicate.

University of Toronto Press acknowledges the financial assistance to its
publishing program of the Canada Council for the Arts and the
Ontario Arts Council.

To all the students who have participated in the work, and whose willing participation, assistance, and encouragement made this handbook possible.

A PART OF YOU IN ME

Every once in a while,
I just sit alone
and think about what happened,
and what's going to happen next.

You left me alone
to face the world by myself.

I just want you to hold me,
but you're not there any more.

I need you here to help me,
I need to feel your presence.

There was always a part of me in you, just as now,
I can still feel
a part of you in me.

— Cory

A little while and I will be gone from among you, whither I go I
cannot tell. From nowhere we came, into nowhere we go. What is life?
It is the flash of a firefly in the night. It is the breath of a buffalo in
the wintertime. It is as the little shadow that runs across the grass and
loses itself in the sunset.

— Crowfoot, Blackfoot Chief, ca. 1890

Contents

Preface

The first bereavement support group in Ontario was formed at Lorne Park Secondary School in Mississauga in 1979, following a grade nine student's tragic death on the tracks of a GO train just south of the school. To our knowledge no such groups were being conducted anywhere in Ontario at that time.

The student's two older sisters, both attending Lorne Park, experienced severe problems following his death. It was their grief that acted as a catalyst to bring together the counselling and nursing services of the school to help them.

School staff had observed that following the death of a family member or close friend or classmate bereaved students often had a great deal of difficulty concentrating in class – or even getting to class. They frequently daydreamed and did not complete homework assignments. Their marks dropped, and they often failed to complete their courses, resulting in added tensions at home, where there were likely many problems already. The school nurse also observed that many bereaved students showed signs of depression, insomnia, weight loss or gain, and other physical complaints considered symptomatic of deeper, underlying problems. Referrals to family doctors usually did not find a physical cause. So the question was asked: 'How can the school help these students?'

Following a meeting that included counselling services staff, the school nurse, and social worker Laurie Bennet, then of the social work department of Mississauga Hospital, plans were implemented to form a bereavement support group program at Lorne Park. All concerned felt that with some extra training, reading, and the help of the psychological services department of the Peel Board of Education, this could be successfully accomplished. In January of 1980, eight bereaved students gathered in the nurse's office in the school, and the first Lorne Park bereavement support group was under way.

The primary purpose of these groups is to help bereaved adolescents work through at least some of the difficulties they are bound to experience following a death. The group provides acceptance and understanding of the grief process by introducing students to others in the same circumstances, others who can help them review the life of the deceased because they have been through the experience themselves and understand what it is to have lost one they loved or deeply cared for. The group is not meant to take the place of the family, but is offered as an addition to the available family support network. Group leaders act as liaisons between students and staff, and organize and plan group meetings. They also assist students in identifying problems so that these can be worked through, if possible.

Professional and practical experience has shown that though the grief of adolescents is similar to that of adults – of course, adults too experience pain, loneliness, guilt, anger, and despair – their grief is compounded by the normal issues of adolescence. They are dealing as well with the additional upheaval caused by their changing bodies, their struggle for independence, and the necessity of making important choices concerning their future. Adolescents also tend to feel misunderstood, and are preoccupied with many unanswered questions. They are looking for advice and comfort, and don't know where to go to get it. Bereavement support groups in the schools can provide such a place.

As one student said, 'I was very uptight when it came to talking about my mom. I was reluctant at first about going to the sessions. I'm relieved now that I chose to go. The group made me feel more comfortable about talking about my mom's death. They answered many of my questions. I was able to talk about my problems and in return I received comforting advice. It wasn't all sad. It's been a really great time.'

Of course such groups cannot be the answer for everyone, and it must be stressed that bereavement groups are not therapy groups. When group leaders recognize that a student needs more than a bereavement group can provide, it is important that he or she be referred for therapy to an outside professional with further training.

This handbook is for caregivers, counsellors, and professionals. It does not contain copious footnotes or detailed clinical observations, but rather relies on our own working knowledge, writings, and research in the field. The material in these pages is meant to offer helpful information and suggestions for those now coping with the ever-increasing problems of grieving adolescents in today's changing society. It was also written to encourage others to seek training in this important area, so that bereavement support group programs for adolescents will continue to expand.

We owe many thanks. Without the enthusiasm, hard work, and dedication of Carol McLean, this handbook would not have been written. Her persistence and encouragement became the catalyst the authors needed to complete the manuscript. We also wish to acknowledge the kind help so freely given by Lois Thomson, who typed several passages for us, Melissa Stuart, who provided and updated the required references, and Andréa Dee, who helped with the editing and preparation. We also owe a debt of gratitude to Laurie Bennett of Hospice of Peel Services, who was so generous with her encouragement. Finally, we wish to thank our copyeditor, Patricia Thorvaldson, for her many helpful suggestions, and Virgil Duff, whose guidance and support made the publication of this handbook possible.

DEATH AND THE ADOLESCENT

1. An Overview

This chapter will familiarize the reader, in brief, with the terminology of grieving and griefwork as well as some of the areas that are helpful to consider before beginning a bereavement group.

Grieving, Mourning, Bereavement

It is generally accepted that the term *grieving* refers to an individual's physical and emotional loss, and describes the way he or she will experience that loss. *Mourning* is the way bereaved people express their feelings of grief, which depends upon factors such as one's religion and culture. In other words, mourning indicates the process which occurs after a loss, a process also called griefwork because mourners must work through their sorrow before the grief can be resolved. *Bereavement*, on the other hand, refers to the total reaction to the loss, and includes both the experience of grief and the work of mourning.

Grief Reactions

Some or all of the factors that follow may be present in the mourning process. In each case their significance will be determined by the individual personality, family structure, and cultural background of the bereaved.

1. Who died (mother, father, child, sibling, grandparent, or another significant person)?

2. The relationship of the family member to the deceased. Obviously, the loss affects each family member differently according to the significance of the relationship to the deceased.
3. How the death occurred:
   - Was it an expected death after a prolonged illness?
   - How well was the family prepared for the death?
   - Was it a sudden and unexpected death?
   - Was the death due to natural causes or to accident, suicide, or murder?
4. The pain involved. Was the death peaceful, pain free, instant, or agonizing? How was it *perceived* by the bereaved?
5. Age of the deceased. We may feel more pain and sorrow around the death of children, young people, and young parents. We tend to accept more readily the death of elderly parents and grandparents, who we might feel have lived to a 'ripe old age.'
6. The relationship of surviving family members to each other, and the ages of the survivors.
7. The number, proximity, and availability of extended family and the relationship with them. The greater the support, the more the bereaved feel people are still caring for them.
8. Other support systems: schools, churches, close friends, neighbours, peers, colleagues, understanding employers, etc.
9. Social, economic, and educational level of the survivors.
10. Necessary changes in family structure, environment, lifestyle, social status, and responsibilities.
11. Self-image of the survivors and the image they present or like to present to others.
12. Social acceptance or nonacceptance of the expression of grief in the bereaved's environment.
13. This is a very important one: COMMUNICATION. Is this a family in which feelings, thoughts, and ideas are expressed openly and decisions affecting the family are discussed beforehand, or do communication problems exist? Are there other family, social, or financial difficulties (extensive debts, problems with health or with the law) that are affecting the surviving family members?

14. Racial and cultural background. What specific worries or problems does each family have?
15. The time of year. Sometimes the date of the death will affect the grief experience by family members, and so the grieving process.

Normal, Reactive Grief

This segment concentrates on the most common grief reactions, those that follow a typical pattern and have both physical and psychological components.

Lindeman (1944) referred to this process as griefwork and described it as involving three major tasks: emancipation from the bondage to the deceased, readjustment to the environment from which the deceased is missing, and the formation of new relationships. Although the major work of grieving is contained within these tasks, James Worden, in *Grief Counselling and Grief Therapy*, makes the valid observation that acceptance of the reality of the loss is an essential last step. This expression of working out of the feelings of grief is the first part of the mourning process. Drawing on the work of both Lindeman and Worden, then, the four tasks of mourning required for healthy resolution can be identified:

Accepting the Reality of the Loss

This concept is much more difficult than it appears, especially in the early stages of grief. In many cases the bereaved person goes on living as though the deceased were still alive: a husband continues to set his deceased wife's place at the dinner table; a bereaved mother waits at the window for her son to return from school.

Letting Go

To let go of a lost relationship the bereaved person has to admit that the loss has occurred – a very slow and painful process.

During this second task, much of the pain of grief is felt, and the bereaved person must learn to face many emotions:

- Shock and numbness. This is often felt early in the grieving process, usually right after hearing of the death, and can result in disbelief or even denial. A bereaved person may also be subject to physical sensations such as feeling light-headed, weak, or sweaty, feelings sometimes accompanied by nausea and vomiting.
- Anguish and depression. As the shock and numbness begin to disappear, the bereaved has to deal with these new, painful feelings. This is the time when one cannot imagine the future and cannot manage in the present.
- Searching behaviour. This term refers to the need of the bereaved to look for and retrieve the lost one, to go over the death again and again. Also, in their memory, they sometimes see the deceased as, say, the perfect father, or their son/daughter as the perfect student.
- Anger. This is a frequent response, directed either at the deceased or at others. For example, the bereaved might say, 'Why did he drive when he had been drinking?'; 'He arrived at the hospital in time; why couldn't the doctors do more?'; or 'Where was God when I needed him?'
- Guilt. Like anger, guilt is felt by most bereaved people: 'If only I had been there, this wouldn't have happened,' or 'Why did I lend her the car?'
- Social withdrawal. Because of the pain of grieving, a bereaved individual will often pull away from social contacts at a time when such support is most needed. Often the grieving person is too depressed to be able to reach out. This is the time when caregivers must come to the rescue.

Adapting to the New Reality

This is the time of painful realization, when one accepts the reality of one's loss and then begins to adapt to new circumstances. It involves the shedding of old habits, learning to adjust to new patterns of interaction, and ultimately changing one's behaviour. This period is often accompanied by intense feelings of guilt by survivors, an indication that their grief is slowly healing.

Going On with Life

This could be called the last stage of griefwork, a stage when the bereaved person feels he or she can reinvest in others and begin to develop a new life. For an adolescent this could mean fulfilling the expectations of, say, a deceased parent, by going to university, studying hard, becoming successful in sports, playing a musical instrument, or in other ways becoming the person the parent hoped he or she might be.

How long does grieving last? It has taken many years for practitioners in the field of griefwork to understand the long-term nature of grief and the recovery process. Until recently, it was thought that grief lasted a year or a year and a half, at which time the mourner would be ready to get on with life. However, practice in the field would indicate that it may be much longer – two or three years, or even more – before a bereaved individual who has suffered the death of a close family member can resume a successful level of functioning. Bereaved individuals have often said that you don't get over it, you just get used to it. Each individual moves at his or her own pace.

Griefwork

People in our culture often try to avoid griefwork by forcing their grief to the back of their minds and going about their daily lives as though nothing has happened. Friends and family often encourage this, with statements such as these:

- 'It is unmanly for men to cry.'
- 'You're taking it so well.'
- 'You shouldn't feel sad; he's out of his suffering now.'
- 'You wouldn't have wanted him to live in pain any longer, would you?'

- 'You must be brave for the children.'
- 'It's God's will.'
- 'You're young and have your whole life ahead of you; you'll meet another.'
- 'You are now the man of the house.'
- 'You must help your father and look after your younger brother.'

It is far better to persevere through *normal griefwork*, which involves:

- Reviewing one's life and experiences; one's memories, hopes, and expectations; and one's relationship with the deceased.
- Going back over the memories of experiences with the lost one and psychologically dealing with these experiences by recognizing and accepting their finality. Memories of course will be both positive and negative. It is hoped that over time the positive memories will outweigh the negative.
- Psychologically 'burying the dead,' or coming to accept the death of the deceased.

Those who are close to the bereaved person can help by:

- Encouraging them to talk about their life with the deceased
- Asking questions about specific experiences they had with the deceased
- Sharing one's own experiences
- Encouraging their tears, and crying with them
- Being with them as their emotions surface and as they talk about their feelings
- When appropriate, moving on to help them form new relationships

Those who have suffered similar losses can be especially helpful because they usually have a greater understanding of what another grieving person is going through. They are also living proof that acute pangs of grief do not last forever, that life does go on, and that there is hope. Further, they are also more likely to be aware of the practical problems that have to be solved, and so are a bridge to help the bereaved form new relationships. That is why it is so important to establish good communication, so that the bereaved know they have someone they can trust and turn to when the need arises.

Sudden Death

Deaths that occur without warning need special understanding. Sudden deaths are usually more difficult to grieve than deaths where there is some prior warning. When dealing with sudden death it is helpful to consider the following factors:

1. Survivors have an exaggerated sense of unreality about the loss. They often feel numb, and they may walk around in a daze for a longer period of time than when the death is anticipated.
2. Guilt feelings are stronger and are often voiced in statements such as
   - 'If only I hadn't done/said such and such.'
   - 'If only I had been with him/had the car fixed/gone myself.'
   - If I had only not given her/him the car.'
   - 'Why did I allow him to buy that motorcycle?'
3. Guilt following a sudden death may be particularly trouble-some in adolescents. They may view the death as the fulfilment of a hostile wish: 'He grounded me, and I wish he were dead!' Adolescents are in the process of achieving emotional and physical separation (autonomy) from parental figures at this time in their lives. They are often hostile to adult authority, and in many cases are also trying to gain control over emerg-ing surges of strong emotions. They are struggling to find their identity.
4. Guilt is also often accompanied by a need to blame someone else for what happened. Thus, it is not unusual for a family member to become the scapegoat. Adolescents and children often become easy targets for such reactions. For example, a surviving parent might blame a family member for failing to

control a situation that has led to the death of another family member.

5. Another feature of sudden death is the involvement of medical and legal authorities, which may cause further complications: often strong hints of culpability leading perhaps to an inquest and in some cases a trial. Or there may be a postmortem, which may take weeks or months and result in no better understanding of the cause of death. Judicial systems also move very slowly, and an investigation may take several years to reach completion. These delays can in turn delay the grieving process, as survivors become distracted by the details surrounding a trial, or while they wait for autopsy results. Of course, these procedures can also be very positive. For example, survivors may get new information that will help them to resolve guilt and/or to place blame in the appropriate place.

6. Survivors may also feel a sense of helplessness, a loss of power and control that is often accompanied by a strong sense of rage. It is not unusual for survivors to vent this anger inappropriately; as a result, hospitals, physicians, governments, other races, etc., may become targets. Occasionally, survivors may even express the wish to kill the person they feel caused the death – an extreme effort to counter the feeling of helplessness.

Suicide

Nearly 750,000 people in the United States commit suicide each year. Survivors are left with a legacy of shame, fear, rejection, anger, and guilt. Dr. Edwin Shneidman, considered to be the father of modern day suicidology in the United States, has stated: 'I believe that the person who commits suicide puts his psychological skeletons in the Survivor's emotional closet. He sentences the survivors to deal with many negative feelings, and more, to become obsessed with thoughts regarding their own actual or possible role in having precipitated the suicidal act or failing to abort it.'

Suicides are among the most difficult bereavement crises for anyone to face and to resolve in any effective manner because of the following factors:

Shame

One of the specific and predominant feelings survivors experience is shame – a result of the stigma attached to suicide. The added emotional pressure can not only affect the survivor's interactions with society, but can also dramatically alter relationships within the family unit. It is not unusual for family members to acknowledge who knows and who does not know the facts surrounding the death, and, almost with tacit agreement, adjust their behaviour towards each other based on this knowledge.

Guilt

Guilt is another common feeling among survivors, who often take responsibility for the action of the deceased and have a growing feeling that there was something they should or could have done to prevent the death. This is particularly true when a suicide happens in the context of some interpersonal conflict.

As we have seen, guilt feelings are normal after any type of death, but in the case of suicide they are usually seriously exacerbated. Because of the intensity of their guilt, people may feel the need to be punished, and so they interact with society in such a way that society in turn does punish them (for example, adolescents who turn to delinquency or drug and alcohol abuse). Some survivors with this need may go to other extremes to get the punishment they think they deserve (overeating to become obese, or otherwise undermining or injuring themselves).

Anger

Survivors may perceive the suicide as a rejection and ask, 'Why?' What they usually mean is 'Why did he/she do this to me?' The intense rage they often experience makes them feel even more guilty. A correlation of this anger is low self-esteem that goes back to feelings of being rejected, the feeling that 'Even death is better than being with me.'

When working with anger in bereavement groups, allowing clients to vent anger freely is most helpful to the grieving process, particularly when the death is a suicide.

Distorted Thinking

Survivors often want to see a death as accidental, not a suicide. When this happens communication in the family becomes distorted. The family effectively creates a myth about the death, and if anyone challenges this myth by calling the death by its real name, they suffer the anger of those who need to see the death as accidental. Myth-making of this kind may be helpful in the short term, but it is not productive in the long run.

When suicide victims come from families in which there are difficult social problems such as alcoholism, drug abuse, and child and spousal abuse, ambivalent feelings probably already exist among family members, and the suicide only serves to exacerbate these feelings and problems.

When dealing with survivors of suicide it is important to realize that others often do not want to hear survivors talk about the death and would prefer that the subject remain unspoken. Here, caregivers can help survivors look at their guilt. Where there is some culpability, survivors will need help accepting the fact that they are human, they make mistakes, and that they need to forgive themselves as much as they can.

Caregivers can help them realize that they are better persons for accepting their part in the death, whether it is something they did or did not do. It is also helpful to redefine the image of the deceased, as many survivors also tend to see victims as all good or all bad, an illusion that needs to be challenged.

Could the deceased really have handled life even with a lot of professional help? Did the deceased have a personality that could have inhibited him or her from succeeding? Does the survivor really believe there was no love or caring at all from the deceased? This kind of reality testing allows the survivor another yardstick with which to judge the deceased objectively, and to correct distorted thinking.

Again, caregivers can help here by maintaining contact and social interaction with survivors, *taking care not to treat them as if they are different,* or that the death is a crime, a stigma, or unmentionable. *These survivors need more help, understanding, sensitivity, and compassion than those grieving any other death.*

The Suicidal Adolescent

As cited in *The Suicide Prevention Handbook*, prepared in 1987 by the Board of Education for the City of Hamilton, recent research has shown that 80 per cent of all suicidal persons give some clues and warnings of their intention. However, it is still extremely difficult to recognize these warnings in adolescents because they often reveal only small pieces of the puzzle, and to different people at different times. As a result it is difficult for any one person to put the pieces together. After a suicide, survivors always ask themselves, 'Why? What could we have done?' or 'Why didn't we take his/her threats more seriously?' *But then sometimes there are just no answers.*

Yes, depressed adolescents thinking of suicide do leave messages and clues as to their intent. But what are these clues? We know that those who have attempted suicide and survived become especially high-risk candidates for another attempt. In some families suicide can be perceived as a legitimate way to escape from intolerable stress.

Studies have shown that suicide often runs in families. The Hemingways are perhaps the best-known example: first, Ernest Hemingway's father; then Hemingway himself; then, in 1997, the author's granddaughter, Margaux. Neither does one need to be mentally ill to consider suicide, or attempt it. Suicide is *a cry for help*, not a selfish desire for attention.

As reported by Ray Corelli, in his article 'Killing the Pain,' in the 29 January 1996 issue of *Maclean's* magazine, Canadian statistics show that from 1979 to 1991 suicides by young people doubled, to 135 per 100,000, ranking Canada third behind New Zealand and Finland. Statistics also point out that although females outnumber males in attempted suicide by a ratio of three to one, it is the males who are more often successful. The male to female ratio of completed suicides is four to one, because of the more lethal methods selected by males. Males tend to choose more violent deaths, by gunshot and hanging, for example, while females prefer poison, pills, and the slashing of wrists. Among adolescents attempting suicide, however, females outnumber males three to one.

Suicide in adolescents is preceded generally by feelings of worthlessness and hopelessness. In fact, it is now widely believed that most suicidal individuals suffer from major depression, and that 80 per cent of suicides could have been prevented with proper drugs and counselling treatment; however, fewer than 20 per cent of all adolescent suicides had received any kind of treatment. Although it is now recognized that some forms of depression are caused by a chemical imbalance in the brain, the condition is very difficult to recognize. Even if treatment is begun, a client is probably looking at one to two years of drug therapy combined with intensive psychiatric counselling before treatment can be deemed effective. Thus, adolescents often feel that no one can do anything about their situation. To them, suicide becomes a way out, or represents the one last bit of control they feel they have over their own lives. It becomes the only way to remove their suffering and emotional pain.

At particularly high risk for this type of behaviour are adolescents who:

- Have tried suicide and failed (reported or not)
- Have been very close to a successful suicide; e.g., a parent, sibling, relative, boyfriend/girlfriend
- Have lost a significant other through death in other ways
- Have had to cope with the breakdown of their family through separation and divorce, or who have had a failed romance, poor relations with their peers, or severe conflicts with their parents
- Exhibit sudden, dramatic changes in their behaviour (such as eating and sleeping patterns)
- Drop out of school, have peer problems, are loners who do not possess effective support networks, or are truant non-attenders with low self-esteem who react to criticism negatively
- Have low or failing grades and test results; or conversely, those who have been categorized as gifted – those to whom anything less than an 'A' represents serious failure, especially if their parents are high achievers; also, students with above-average IQs who are seriously underachieving both in school

and in life (a group that includes students with 'learning dis-
abilities,' especially if they have gone undiagnosed)
• Have problems with alcohol and substance abuse
• Have been sexually abused and/or who are pregnant
• Are engaging in unnecessary risk-taking, such as speeding, or
  have become preoccupied with thoughts of dying; students
  who only listen to 'satanic' types of music or who are writing
  stories or poetry about death
• Begin to give away their prized possessions to friends, indicating that they won't need them anymore (e.g., records, light-
  ers, watches, skateboards, etc.)
• Start to give their peers hints that they are 'thinking about it,'
  or are thinking about going on a trip

The Coroner's Office

The coroner must investigate all deaths that cannot be explained.
Adolescents are sometimes unaware that they have the right to
the coroner's findings, and sometimes to police reports as well.
Counsellors have often noted that there is a great deal of mystery, misinformation, and speculation concerning some deaths.
Many survivors feel it is best to protect adolescents from such
information. However, providing that adolescents have the legal
right to the facts in a particular case, it is often helpful to obtain
such information by making an appointment with the local coroner. The truth, difficult as it might be, is usually better than not
knowing the facts surrounding an unexplained death, or being
denied information.

When Bodies Cannot Be Recovered

When the body of a deceased person cannot be recovered, the
potential for denial is greater than usual. For most bereaved, it is
most important to see the body of the deceased. The physical
presence of the body allows the bereaved person to better see
the connection between life and death. Thus, in cases of disaster
– air crashes, war, murder, etc. – when the body cannot be recov-

ered, it is even more difficult for the bereaved person to believe that the person truly has died. The presence of the body allows the funeral rites and then the mourning process to begin.

Funeral Services

Today, many funeral homes have skilled and caring bereavement counsellors or staff who are willing to help families with short-term, uncomplicated bereavement counselling. These establishments offer in-service sessions for schools and the community, and often possess excellent resources (libraries, tapes, etc.) which they will lend to interested members of the public. They are staffed with helpful, caring people who respect the feelings and religious beliefs of all, and want to be of service to families during their bereavement crisis. Funeral staff are often very knowledgeable about their community, and wish to support many community concerns.

Thoughts on Adolescent Development

Teachers, counsellors, and all caregivers recognize that adolescence is a difficult period. It is a time often characterized by struggles between dependence (on parents) and independence. Adolescence is also marked by a desire to abandon childhood patterns, though adolescents may be frightened as well to become adults. This is also a time when adolescents are undergoing immense physical changes and must come to grips with many social changes in their lives as well. During this period teenagers experience intense and sometimes frightening and upsetting mood swings, which may make the death of a parent or any significant other an even more devastating experience.

Most adolescents have intense relationships with their siblings (not always of a positive nature), which often involve bitter rivalry. Although this can be quite normal, if a brother or sister dies suddenly the remaining sibling is often left with feelings of guilt and a sense that there is unfinished business to deal with. This complicates the experience of mourning. Some adolescents have been known to be so frightened by experiences of this kind that they have believed they were 'going crazy.'

Adolescents also experience a very difficult time if they have lost a girlfriend or a boyfriend. Because of their often heightened feeling of love, when this kind of death occurs (for example, sudden death in an automobile accident) the survivor is faced with intense feelings of isolation and helplessness. As we have seen, these adolescents also warrant special attention because of their potential risk for suicide.

Adolescents must deal also with the physical and emotional changes related to their sexuality. This can mean not only a range of conflicting emotions, but perhaps the issues of pregnancy, sexual desire (including the risk of sexually transmitted diseases), sexual identity, and the ever-present host of dating rituals. Physically, both sexes are faced with their emerging body images. If the adolescent is not comfortable with his or her body, this may trigger acne, obesity, anorexia nervosa, or bulimia.

School pressures, coupled with the pressure to obtain good grades in order to enter a favourite college or university, are additional stressors for adolescents. Schools today are also plagued with the constant problems created by substance abuse and by peer pressure with its codes of conformity and subsequent fears of rejection.

Teenagers also face family breakdown through separation and divorce (statistics suggest close to 50 per cent), and in many cases they have become the victims of physical, sexual, and mental abuse within the family.

Throughout all this physical and emotional strife, adolescents must begin to develop their own value system, which will allow them to develop a sense of personal identity. When this is accomplished they will feel more secure within their own peer groups, and more confident with members of the opposite sex. Later, they will hopefully have the ability to respond positively to the society around them so that successful career and life choices can be made.

When a parent dies, adolescents sometimes lose not only one parent but two, as the surviving parent copes with his or her own grief. This is often true as well when a sibling dies, leaving the surviving adolescent with no one to talk to. Thus, adolescents do benefit a great deal from their own grief groups, ones in which they are free to express their own feelings and where they can find acceptance. In such groups, adolescents have permission to grieve, they learn that their feelings are normal, and they discover that the intensity of their grief will not last forever. Here, grieving is allowed to take place within structures and boundaries and with sympathetic adults and empathetic peer leaders, giving adolescents a chance to reach some resolution to their pain.

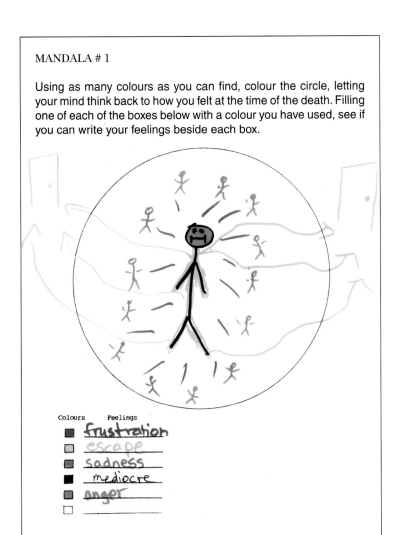

MANDALA # 1

Using as many colours as you can find, colour the circle, letting your mind think back to how you felt at the time of the death. Filling one of each of the boxes below with a colour you have used, see if you can write your feelings beside each box.

Colours   Feelings

■ frustration
□ escape
■ sadness
■ mediocre
■ anger
□

Two months following his father's suicide a 17-year-old used a mandala to express his grief.

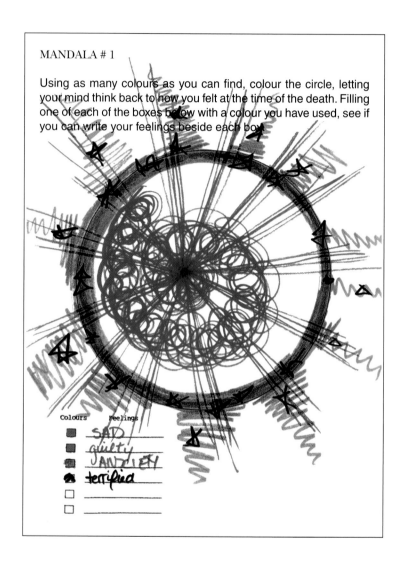

MANDALA # 1

Using as many colours as you can find, colour the circle, letting your mind think back to how you felt at the time of the death. Filling one of each of the boxes below with a colour you have used, see if you can write your feelings beside each box

Colours   Feelings

SAD

guilty

ANXIEN

terrified

A 14-year-old girl drew this mandala six months after the death of her mother.

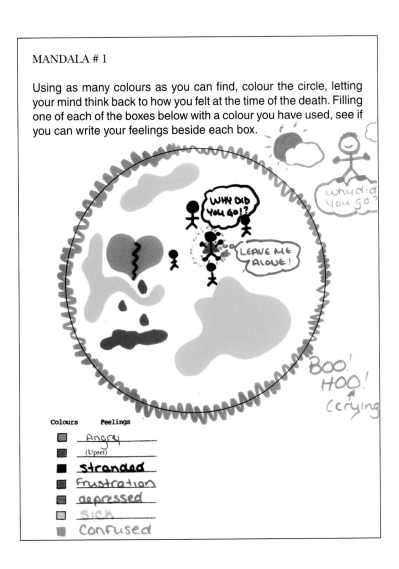

MANDALA # 1

Using as many colours as you can find, colour the circle, letting your mind think back to how you felt at the time of the death. Filling one of each of the boxes below with a colour you have used, see if you can write your feelings beside each box.

Colours Peelings

- Angrey
- (Upset)
- stranded
- Frustration
- depressed
- sick
- Confused

Four years after the death of her brother a 15-year-old expressed her grief in this mandala.

MANDALA # 1

Using as many colours as you can find, colour the circle, letting
your mind think back to how you felt at the time of the death. Filling
one of each of the boxes below with a colour you have used, see if
you can write your feelings beside each box.

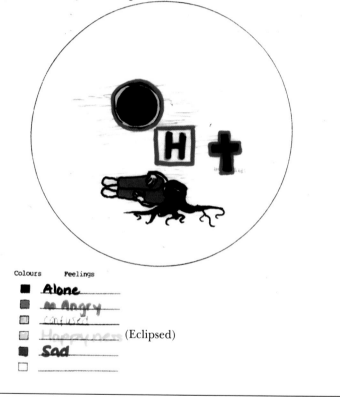

Colours   Feelings
■ Alone
■ An Angry
▨ Confused
▨ Happyness (Eclipsed)
■ Sad
☐

A 14-year-old was unaware that her father would not survive a long-term
illness in hospital; mandala completed four months after his death.

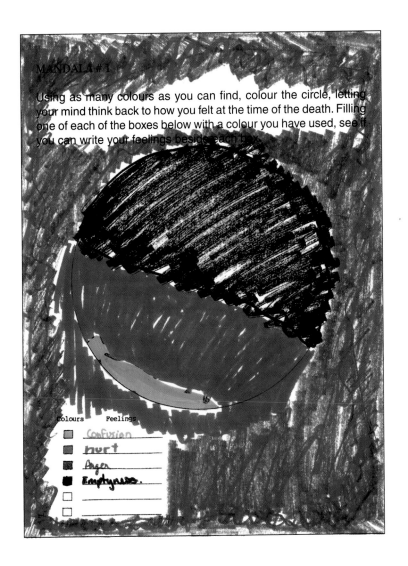

MANDALA # 1

Using as many colours as you can find, colour the circle, letting your mind think back to how you felt at the time of the death. Filling one of each of the boxes below with a colour you have used, see if you can write your feelings beside each box.

Colours   Feelings

☐ Confusion
☐ hurt
☐ Anger
■ Emptyness.
☐ _____
☐ _____

A 14-year-old drew this mandala during group session four years after her brother's suicide.

For the last month of his life, following a long-term illness, a father was unable to communicate with his 17-year-old daughter; mandala completed during group session, four months after his death.

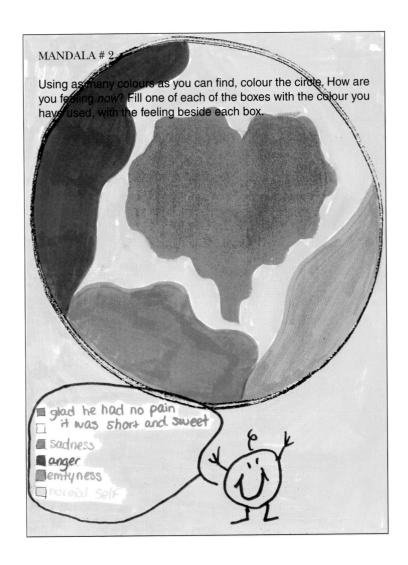

A 15-year-old boy, in his second-last group session, one year after his father died on a ski slope of a heart attack.

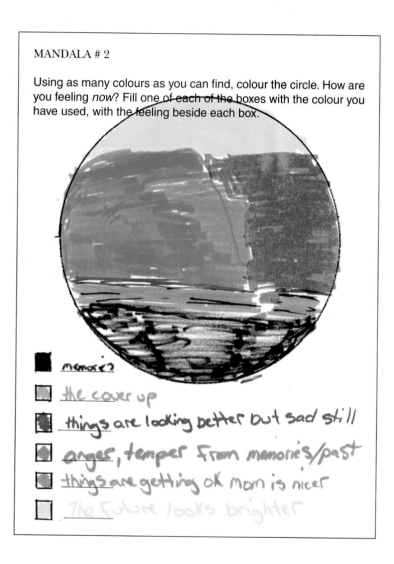

MANDALA # 2

Using as many colours as you can find, colour the circle. How are you feeling *now*? Fill one of each of the boxes with the colour you have used, with the feeling beside each box.

■ memores?

■ the cover up

■ things are looking better but sad still

■ anger, temper from memories/past

■ things are getting ok mom is nicer

■ The future looks brighter

A 14-year-old girl, in her second-last group session, eight months after her stepfather died of cancer.

2. *Forming a Group*

This chapter focuses on the grief groups themselves. It first offers, in brief, some of the theory associated with grief counselling and the stages of group dynamics. The bulk of the chapter takes the reader step by step through the ten sessions that comprised one primary adolescent support group, including sample exercises and detailed responses from group members. Readers are encouraged to use it as a guide towards creating their own unique adolescent bereavement groups.

Group Support/Grief Counselling

It is important, once again, to distinguish between the normal grief process – one that allows counsellees to complete the normal grieving tasks within a reasonable time frame – and abnormal or complicated grief reactions – those that should be dealt with by qualified mental health professionals who have completed further training in bereavement counselling: psychologists, psychiatrists, and social workers.

It is extremely important, as well, that group leaders have at least some training themselves in group psychotherapy, so that they are able to distinguish between adolescents who are suitable for their groups, and those who need additional help. Effective leaders of course must also be capable of establishing a supportive, warm, nonthreatening, and trusting environment. Adolescents can be quick to recognize ineffective, authoritarian, confrontational leaders who show little respect or empathy. Because of the emotional nature of bereavement counselling, co-leaders are especially recommended. This allows one leader to concentrate on issues while the other deals with process, and vice versa. Of course, counsellors who are themselves psychologically healthy, and who have a capacity to form deep, trusting relationships with others, will get the best results. Needless to say, bereavement counselling is not for the faint-hearted.

Before beginning a group, it is a good idea to read as much as possible of the current literature, material that discusses bereavement counselling and practice, as well as theory and group dynamics. It is helpful also to volunteer in the palliative care programs of local hospitals, where further hours of instruction and practical work can be experienced. Lastly, enroll in recognized programs in fields that deal with life-threatening illness and with dying, and bereavement. Certification in the primary areas of school counselling and nursing can only be more beneficial to the work.

The Four Stages of Group Dynamics

As has been suggested, those practitioners who wish to enter this field do have an obligation to seek training in this area. However, the following notes will give practitioners a brief overview of this very complicated topic.

It is important to realize that all groups move through four stages: a beginning or exploratory stage, a transition stage, an action stage, and a termination stage. Group leaders must be familiar with these stages in order to help counsellees move from one stage to another.

1. The Exploratory Stage

In the beginning leaders should strive to build a trusting relationship so that members can risk disclosure. It is at this stage that the group establishes its norms and consciously or unconsciously assigns power and influence to each member. At this point leaders should model the facilitative characteristics of empathy, warmth, respect, and genuineness.

2. The Transition Stage

At this point, more counsellees will begin to self-disclose at a level beyond the superficial. This stage requires a great deal of sensitivity on the part of group leaders, as counsellees must be able to give responses that are at least minimally action-oriented.

3. The Action Stage

Here, group leaders must work with their group members towards the belief that their condition will change if they are willing to take a risk. 'Homework' is also assigned at this stage, and group members are asked to report back to the group concerning their progress or lack thereof. Group members may confront one another, but group leaders should always be aware that they are the gatekeepers of the group's safety. Be patient.

While there is sometimes a nonparticipator in a group, leaders must not despair. Bereaved adolescents do seem to benefit simply from the group process itself (see student responses, p. 43). The prognosis for success varies from counsellee to counsellee and from group to group. The more responsive adolescents are, the more they will feel they have benefited from the group experience.

4. The Termination Stage

This stage slowly signals to the group that the time for self-disclosure is coming to an end. It is a time when group participants must decide what the group has meant to them, and, finally, whether or not they plan to reunite at a later date. Hopefully, the group has given participants an opportunity to work through their difficulties and differences, and to grow.

It should be noted that group dynamics do not necessarily flow evenly from one stage to another. Leaders must remain flexible and be willing simply to go where the group wants to go. Leaders should always remember, as well, that the group exists for the group members, not for the leaders, that these are 'support' groups only, although any bereavement group will also serve a therapeutic purpose.

It should be noted, too, that bereavement groups will not resolve all adolescents' grief reactions. The tasks of grieving cannot be completed after just ten sessions, though there is no question that these groups always resolve at least some of the tasks of mourning so that these adolescents can reach some resolution in their lives. Being part of a bereavement group not only allows teenagers to deal with the pain of grief, it also encourages them to seek help, if needed, in the future.

One final – and most important – consideration: these groups cannot involve both adolescents and parents. Experience has shown that attempts to work with parents have resulted in the adolescents feeling betrayed. Although most grieving adolescents want to help their grieving parents, they also feel that if you support their parents' grief you cannot support theirs. Adolescent bereavement groups work best if the young people work together to help each other.

The Three Basic Groups

Although the group process remains the same, three distinct and different types of groups have been identified, each group serving a different purpose. (See also step 7, p. 25.)

The Primary Adolescent Support Group

This group is the primary focus of our work and the model on which the other two groups are based. Participating in this group are the adolescents who have lost an immediate member of their family such as a parent, sibling, or, in some cases, a very significant other such as a boyfriend/girlfriend, or very loving grandparents who have lived within the family unit and perhaps have acted as surrogate parents for the bereaved adolescent(s). However, adolescents bring the experience of all types of death to this group including suicide, murder, and the horror of war and genocide.

The Grandparents Group

This group deals only with the death of grandparents. Adolescents are often very close to their grandparents, especially if they are privileged to have had extensive contact with them (not a common occurrence in present-day society). This group usually consists of five or six sessions.

The Peer Group

Adolescents are especially touched by the death of a peer, and their grief over this loss is especially intense. Because adolescents obtain great support from their peers (who perhaps have not yet experienced a death), bereavement groups can be very beneficial for them. These groups are much more informal: for example, members might meet during lunch hours, and their composition may change from session to session (three or four in total). Here peers review and remember the life of the deceased, and try to find answers for deaths often caused by terminal illness, or tragic events such as automobile accidents, drowning, and suicide. (See also 'The Suicidal Adolescent,' p. 13; and 'Planning a Memorial Service,' p. 79.)

Getting a Group Started

The following twelve steps outline the procedures required before a group can be formed.

1. Seek the permission and support of the principal and staff of the school. If possible, give a brief presentation to explain that a bereavement group will be starting, and why and when students will need to be absent from class.
2. Plan to have two leaders present for every group. This is very important. One leader will be needed to look for 'effective'

statements, while the other looks after 'instrumental' questions. (Effective statements are those that evolve from the adolescents' intense feelings; instrumental responses are merely statements of time and place.) Because of the emotional drain that can result from this type of counselling, it is important that leaders also have backup support from others, such as the school psychologist or social worker.

3. Identify students who are candidates for the group, with a view to starting the group at least three months after the deaths have occurred). The waiting period allows adolescents to get over the shock and numbness usually felt in the early stages following a death. (It is important to remember that adolescents can benefit from these groups even many years after a death of a family member or other significant person in their lives.)

The recommended number of members for any one group is six to eight. If a greater number of bereaved students are identified, it is preferable to plan a separate group. (It has been surprising and shocking to discover that numbers of bereaved students in one school can be high: for example, in an average-sized secondary school of 1,400 students, 20 were found to be bereaved.) Note, too, that counsellors have attempted from time to time to include students from other schools, but because of transportation problems these efforts have usually failed.

4. Invite each potential group member to an individual interview with both group leaders. To explain the purpose of the group and to outline what will be expected of its members, leaders should follow this procedure:
   – Welcome the student, mention the death, and express condolences.
   – Ask questions: Who died? When did the death occur? How close was the relationship?
   – Tell the students about the group and how others have felt about the experience. Stress that the group offers support, not therapy; that members may simply listen or they may share their experiences, whichever they prefer. Inform them that their teachers will be notified about the

group, but will not be told what happens or is said during the sessions.

   – Outline the practical aspects: the group schedule, the importance of being on time, etc.

5. Following the interview:
   – Establish a list of participants and notify teachers of the time of the sessions. (See sample teacher notification form, p. 54.)
   – Locate a quiet, informal room with carpet or pillows on the floor; a place *with no opportunity for interruptions.*
   – Contact parent(s) by letter (see permission form, p. 53) informing them of the group, indicating that their son/daughter wishes to participate, and offering to discuss any concerns they may have. Depending on the particular situation, counsellors might ask for formal permission for the students to participate. Students under the age of 16 should have consent from a guardian, though older participants should be encouraged to tell their guardians about the groups, and that group leaders would welcome any inquiries.

6. It is strongly recommended that support groups be held during school hours for the following practical reasons:
   – The group then becomes a natural part of the school day.
   – Students have their own after-school commitments, such as jobs, looking after younger siblings, sports and school activities. Not all students have access to a car, and school transportation is not always available. Often parents feel that homework should be done during the evening, and want students to remain at home.
   – It is crucial that the adolescent be allowed to grieve and to recognize that his or her own peers are facing the same problems.
   – The group is an adolescent support group that should be held in an appropriate adolescent setting such as the school (open to their peers only).

7. Group composition is also very important. It has been found that all ages and both sexes mix well from grades nine through thirteen. However, it is important to deal only with

the deaths of immediate family members and boyfriends/ girlfriends in one group, and *the deaths of grandparents not living in the home in another group*, as the problems differ greatly. This also allows for the differences in intense feelings between 'close' relations and those that are 'not so close.' As group leaders, we soon found that grandparents occupy a special place in a teenager's heart. Grandparents are special, they often are not faced with the day-to-day problems of disciplining unruly teens, and, unfortunately, are often a young person's first experience with death. Thus, allowing teens to grieve for their grandparents gives young people the opportunity to work through their grief in a supportive manner. However, if the grandparent was the *sole support giver* for that student, he or she should be placed in the regular eight-to-ten-session group. Again, grandparents groups should consist of eight to ten students per group, and should usually last approximately five sessions compared to a usual group of eight to ten sessions. The authors have also discovered that *siblings should be asked* if they wish to be part of the same group. Sometimes this does work, though other times it would have been more beneficial if each had been in a separate group. The composition of each group will be different, and the willingness of members to share experiences will vary with each group.

One example of a scenario in which separation might be encouraged is in the case of severe sibling rivalry. However, if siblings are in the same group, the leaders should be aware that, depending on their age and relationship to the deceased, different opinions or stories will emerge. In all cases where students *choose* to remain in a specific group it has been a positive learning experience for all parties. Again, as a general rule these decisions are best left to the adolescents themselves.

8. Peer counselling has been very helpful because students who have participated in a group will often volunteer to help others, especially immediately after a death and before a new group forms. Peer counsellors can also help those students who do not want to be part of a group but neverthe-

less need support. Former group graduates have often been included as peer co-leaders, with great success. Peer co-leaders often ask the 'right questions,' and give their peers permission to 'tell it like it is.' Peer support can also be enhanced within the group through the exchange of telephone numbers and through networking over vacation periods such as Christmas or March break. Often, older students will 'adopt' a younger member of the group and take the role of big sister or brother, thus giving peer support to their new friend. Peer counselling definitely adds a great deal to groups and helps the process of group cohesion.

9. When a parent has died, it has been helpful at times, *with the student's permission*, to share the concerns of the counsellee with the remaining parent. This often has resulted in an increase in home support, or perhaps further professional help for the adolescent and his/her family. It has also improved communication in the home with the surviving parent. Such outreach by the school has always been valued.

10. Over time, leaders and group members have found that afternoon meetings are best. This time fits in with the school timetable and students only miss the last period of the day, usually from 2 P.M. to 3 P.M. As a result, with their rotating class schedules, students are only absent from half of the last class. This is very intensive counselling for students and leaders, so it is good that they do not have to return to the classroom. It also gives the leaders time to *record the sessions* after the students have departed.

11. Immediately after all sessions, it is important that co-leaders review what happened in the group, noting the concerns of each member of the group and any key statements or information each contributed. *It definitely helps to keep a log after each meeting that includes a short note about each student.* The log thus becomes a record of each group session. It helps leaders remember who died, and how, and keep track of which issues are important for each counsellee. Using a log, leaders can then formulate a plan for each session; for example, how to draw out the silent counsellee or to ask a question that will stimulate discussion or clarify a statement. (See also

Sample Logs, p. 45.) Keeping a log of each session also gives the leaders a chance to review the group process as the group is moving through the different stages (problem-solving, transition, etc.).

12. Co-leaders should meet prior to each session to plan the 'agenda' and try to anticipate any problems that may occur. For example, if a student breaks down during the first session and wants to leave the group, one of the leaders should be prepared to leave with the student and later, hopefully, to encourage him or her to return to the group. Co-leaders should also send out notices of each session to participants, and arrange for refreshments. Once the sessions begin, have a box of tissues close by at all times.

The Ten Sessions

This section outlines each of the ten sessions in further detail, and illustrates some of the aids or helpful hints counsellors might consider when conducting adolescent bereavement groups.

One of the most important tools in the group process is the mandala. A powerful symbol since ancient times, it has been a symbol of the universe used as an aid to religious meditation, and more recently – particularly as conceived by psychologist Carl Jung – it has been a symbol representing the wholeness of the self. In Jung's view, 'the spontaneous production of a mandala is a step in the individuation process and ... represents an attempt by the conscious self to integrate hitherto unconscious material.'[1]

In the experience of many co-leaders the use of mandalas to help group members express their feelings in a non-threatening manner has been particularly useful. It has been enlightening to see how young people use colours to release and relieve their feelings. All students seem to enjoy this exercise regardless of any 'artistic' ability. For some adolescents it is less easy to share with group members the meaning of their drawings and colours.

---

1 *New Encyclopedia Britannica*, 15th ed., s.v. 'Mandala.'

Still, most have truly enjoyed explaining their finished mandalas, and many have commented on how much this part of the group work had helped them.

Mandala 1 (from Session 2)

The examples of Mandala 1, following page 18, illustrate the feelings often expressed by bereaved adolescents in the months immediately following the death of a family member, friend, or other significant person. Observing these early mandalas, it can be seen that the harsher colours are expressing feelings such as hurt, confusion, depression, anger, and rage.

The other sample exercises given here – Images; Memories; Problems Happening to Me Now; and Things You Wish You Had Done or Said – are additional tools to encourage reluctant counsellees to express their grief. They might not be needed.

The ten sessions that follow illustrate the bereavement group process as a whole, and describe many of the issues bereaved adolescents present to their groups. Co-leaders should consider the material primarily as a guide. Each bereavement group is unique, and co-leaders are encouraged to make their groups their own.

Session 1: Beginning Stage or Introduction

This is one of the most difficult sessions for both leaders and counsellees. Be prepared for strong emotions, including anger, mistrust, etc., directed towards anyone in the group, as well as some tears. To establish comfort:

- Pick a quiet, comfortable room.
- Sit in a circle, on chairs or on the floor.
- Have co-leaders sitting among the students, not together.
- Begin the group process by having a group leader share a death experience, to help set the tone for the group.
- Reassure the group that everyone feels nervous and uncomfortable at first, but that they will all soon become friends.
- Serve simple refreshments.

- Use first names.
- Encourage the students to briefly tell their story.
- Emphasize the rule of confidentiality.
- Give permission to 'pass' if someone is not ready to talk.
- Give permission to cry, and have tissues readily available.
- Accept students' feelings with reflective listening.

Sharing information and feelings is a vital process in helping students to:

- Know they are not alone
- Know what is considered 'normal' when one is grieving
- Explore feelings by establishing links with other members
- Gain support from others
- Gain insight even if he or she is a quiet member of the group (Even if not acknowledged, or the student is in denial, the message does get through.)

At the conclusion of the session:

- Reinforce the rules for attendance and each person's responsibility for notifying the leader in advance if he or she cannot attend.
- Remind students about confidentiality, concerning themselves, their parents, group leaders, and peers.
- Encourage students to attend regularly, as a help not only to themselves but to the whole group.
- Record all observations in a log.

Session 2: Feelings/Mandala 1

- Remember to bring mandalas, coloured markers, and paper for recording telephone numbers.
- Begin the group by asking each adolescent to retell his or her story, this time with more details. This retelling is often very different from the story as told in the first session. For example, what was first called a 'nice' death can suddenly become a suicide.

- This is a time to discuss the circumstances surrounding each death: treatment in the hospital, anger at hospital staff, accidents, the notice reporting the death, physical and psychological changes of the person who died (for example, from cancer, etc.).
- This is definitely the *last time to add a new member* since group cohesion will already have taken place.
- Distribute mandala 1 (see sample, page 32) to counsellees, with these instructions:

'This is an exercise in using colour to express your feelings. Using as many colours as you wish to colour your mandala, let your mind think back to how you felt at the time of the death. See if you can write your feelings beside the colours you have used.'

- When the mandalas are completed, ask each counsellee in turn to hold up his or her mandala and explain the feelings expressed there. Some members may need encouragement from the leaders.
- Encourage counsellees to talk with one another if they need extra support before the next session.
- Complete the exchange list with leaders' and group members' telephone numbers.
- Leaders complete their log.

Session 3: Beginning the Transition Stages – Funerals/Wakes

- Begin by asking if anyone has anything more they would like to talk about from Session 2.
- Explain that the whole of Session 3 is to be used to talk about funerals, cremation, and/or burial. It is important for leaders to remember this information in future (via leaders' notes) because in our multicultural society customs differ. (See Appendix 1.)
- During the discussion leaders should keep in mind that adolescents often become very angry with some of the ritual of funerals: some believe much of the process is barbaric. For

Mandala 1, Session 2

Using as many colours as you can find, colour the circle, letting
your mind think back to how you felt at the *time of the death*. See
if you can write your feelings beside the colours you have used.

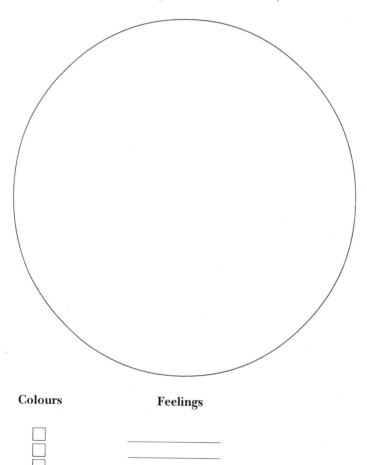

Colours   **Feelings**

some of the counsellees this could be their first funeral with an open casket, and viewing a body can be a very frightening experience.

- Remember as well that many students may have angry feelings about how a specific funeral was conducted – for example, whether the deceased was buried or cremated – especially if they were allowed no input. Everyone will have different customs and experiences, so leaders should be prepared to hear a variety of opinions.
- To prepare for Session 4, remind students to bring photographs or other reminders – treasures, keepsakes – of the deceased.
- Leaders complete their log.

Session 4: The Deceased/Suicide Check

- Remind counsellees that this session's focus is remembering those who have died. Check that everyone has brought a photograph or other memento. If some students forget to bring photographs, suggest that they bring one to a later session.
- Ask each group member in turn to talk about his or her photograph or keepsake. Leaders should try to encourage both *good and bad memories*, so that the 'whole person' can be seen. (See also Part 2 of Exercise 4, p. 35.)
- Do a suicide check. Because teens often believe they are immortal, they may engage in risk-taking behaviour. Therefore, it is extremely important for group leaders to realize that adolescents may fantasize about joining the deceased. A suicide check during the transition stage of the group will help. On occasion, leaders have felt it necessary to refer a high-risk candidate for outside psychotherapy to a practitioner who specializes in bereavement counselling. Such individuals remain in the group but receive additional individual therapy outside the group. Both interventions complement each other.
- For additional information to use in this session, see 'Suicide,' p. 10; also 'The Suicidal Adolescent,' p. 13.

Exercise 4 for Session 4 (Aids for Group Leaders)

Images

If you do not have a picture, draw something which reminds you of the person you have lost. Would you like to create a poem for the person who died?

Exercise 4 for Session 4, Part 2

Memories

My three **best** memories are:

1.

2.

3.

My three **worst** memories are:

1.

2.

3.

Session 5: Beginning of Problem-Solving

This session's focus is on the ways death has changed the lives of group members, and on the new problems they may be experiencing. Leaders should also refer to Common Problems, p. 55, and Exercise 5, p. 37.

Discussion with counsellees could include the following topics:

* Failing grades at school and parents' reaction; trying to get into college or university
* Increased household responsibilities – taking on new roles
* Discipline or lack thereof in the home
* Introduction of a new partner for a widowed parent; new stepbrothers/sisters
* Health problems; drugs; alcohol
* Financial worries; selling the house; money for post-secondary education
* Dealing with fears: the cemetery, urns in the house, hallucinations/going crazy
* Leaders complete log.

Session 6: Action Stage (1)

This is a problem-solving session that continues through sessions 7 and 8. Some points to consider:

* Who or what helped, both at the time of the death and now? Ask for examples.
* What or who did not help? One example might be the adult at the funeral or visitation who said the adolescent must now be the 'man or woman of the family.'
* Set up a group folder and invite group members to write questions or give suggestions to the group anonymously. These questions can then be used by leaders to stimulate the group if discussion wanes.
* Continue discussions from Exercise 5, p. 37.
* Leaders complete log.

Exercise 5 for Sessions 5, 6

Problems happening to me now or how my life has changed

At school (eg., failing grades):

At home (eg., increased household duties, discipline [or lack of discipline], remaining parent/brother(s), sister(s), parent's 'new' partner):

Money problems (selling the house, money for college):

Problems with my friends:

Health problems:

Session 7: Action Stage (2)

- Adolescents listen to conversations and sometimes get the wrong information. Encourage them to go back to their families and ask! The bereavement group does not take the place of family support.
- Encourage communication. For example, both parents of one young man were killed in a car accident. He had to leave his home, school, friends, and his dog, and live with his brother and his young family in another city. He had a number of problems in the home and group members encouraged him to talk things over with his brother, not to keep them bottled up. Sometimes adolescents who do not get enough love at home will seek 'love' through sex, thereby creating more problems. If leaders are brave, a discussion concerning the use/abuse of drugs/alcohol might be introduced here.

Session 8: Action Stage (3)

- Encourage counsellees to write poems or create stories about the deceased. These may or may not be shared with the group depending on the wishes of the participant.
- Encourage the discussion of dreams or nightmares, especially those that are recurring. Remembering dreams and nightmares can make the grief process a lot harder, but if these are discussed openly and adolescents are given some strategies to deal with them, it can help. For example, a daughter dreams again and again of her father drowning. Why? He was a good swimmer. She is also a good swimmer, a lifeguard. If she had been there, she feels she would have saved him. The body of her father was unrecognizable after being in the water three weeks. To some extent, this counsellee still believes it wasn't him. Still, this verbally expressed belief was contradicted by her mandala on which she had colored in deep blue water.

  Another group member came to the school every morning for a week to talk to her group leader about a terrible recurring nightmare in which her mother lay decaying in the ground. The counsellor tried to use imagery to help her. She suggested the girl place a photograph of her mother by her bed so that she could see it when she awoke from her nightmare; and that she turn on some music to break the pattern of the nightmare in her mind.

- Leaders reminder to bring mandala 2 to the next session.
- Leaders complete log.

Session 9: Termination/Mandala 2

By Session 9 it is hoped that the counsellees' mandalas are now more positive and the colours more uplifting. Perhaps the feelings expressed exhibit some resolution of their grief and pain. The messages sometimes reflect that significant resolution has taken place. (See examples of Mandela 2 following page 18.) In fact, the completion of the second mandala often signals that group counselling has come to an end.

- Remind everyone of the limited time left in the group.
- Have everyone do another mandala to ascertain what *their feelings are now*. Again, ask each counsellee to explain his/her mandela briefly.
- Suggest strategies to help with remaining anger: punching a pillow; running or other exercise; talking with someone instead of punching walls or fighting with teachers.
- Suggest that students complete self-help exercise 9 (p. 41). Remind them that this is a personal exercise for counsellees that does not need to be shared with anyone, and that the finished exercise can be placed in their personal files with their mandalas.
- Remind students that only one session remains, and ask if anyone has anything more that needs to be said.
- Leaders complete log.

Session 10: Closing

- Ask each adolescent to evaluate the group (see questionnaire p. 42).
- Serve pizza and pop or otherwise create a party-like atmosphere to help group members say goodbye. Be sure everyone

Mandala 2, Session 9

Again, using as many colours as you wish, complete this mandala now that you have almost finished the group sessions. Try to reassess how you feel *now* about the death. Write your feelings beside the colours you used.

Colours   **Feelings**

How do the colours differ from the first mandala? Are your feelings any different?

Exercise 9 for Session 9

Things you wish you had done for or said to the person who died

1.

2.

3.

4.

Session 10

Sample Wrap-Up Questionnaire:

This sample questionnaire is completed by all group members (Session 10).

NAME (optional):_____

Please be as honest as you can.

1. How has this group been helpful to you?

2. What did you expect of the group that did not happen?

3. Suggestions for future groups.

☐ Check here if you would be interested in providing peer support to someone coping with death.

has leaders' and members' phone numbers so that they can keep in touch. Remind the adolescents that it is a good idea to keep in contact with one another, and that group leaders are always available to them.

* Leaders complete log.
* At a later date, leaders can evaluate the group by means of the student questionnaire (see also the following samples of student responses).

Typical Student Responses

The following is a sample of the responses turned in by students on the student evaluation forms.

'It's a great help to have someone to turn to if you just can't make it through the day by yourself. When you are in a group situation such as the one I was in, you learn that you aren't so different from everybody else and that most people also experience what you go through. The group provides a reassuring atmosphere that can be very important when you may be going through a particularly hard week.'   — Andrew

'I feel the group provides a special bond between the members in it because even if you pass by a group member in the hall and you don't say anything, you know they know how you feel, and that if you were upset you could talk to them at any time. The group helps you understand your own feelings and other people's feelings. This helps you to be able to help yourself and hopefully to be a help to another member.'   — Barbara

'The group sessions were introduced at a time when I needed contact with other people with similar emotional upsets. They have helped me to talk more freely on the subject of death and its impact on my family and myself and others. Being able to discuss it openly with others has relieved tension and pain. With the discussions in the group I have found it easier to talk with others in my family; in this way it has helped not only me but my mother and sister cope with the stresses and strains.'   — Janet

'The program has helped me a great deal and I hope it will continue to help others.'   — Anita

'When my sister died I was accused of not showing feelings. They were right. I shut up everything inside me and became a listener. Group has made it easier for me to talk, though I didn't talk a lot. I became aware of a couple of things. Firstly, that I was a listener and have a lot of violence shut up inside me. Secondly, that the reason I was quieter in nature was I didn't understand the feelings inside me. I felt alone and different.

'You group members have made me understand myself better. I thank you a million times over, at least.'   — Sincerely, Jon

'The group helped me in the following ways: If I had a problem similar to one of the other group members but was too shy to say it, I could learn from them how to cope with it. It helped me accept the death in my family.'   — Carol

'The group has helped a great deal, not only by helping me realize that you can't bring back the past, but also finally making me accept the fact that he's gone, and nothing I or anyone else can do will bring him back. No matter how much you want that to happen. Also when you see other members in the hall or in class, you think that if they are managing, then so can you, and just knowing that you are not the only one with a problem helps. Sometimes when you're feeling low, it is nice to know that you have somewhere to go and can talk to someone your age. I would seriously recommend a person who is trying to cope with a problem such as this to join a group. It does HELP.'   — L.B.

One response was this poem written by a daughter to her deceased mother. The poem was read to the group.

AN IMAGINARY PLACE

There is an imaginary place
Deep within my head
When I am lying in Bed.
This place is wherever I want it to be

But I always have one place in mind
This place is called 'Heaven'
Where I have lost someone so kind.
I sometimes wish it wasn't imaginary
That I could really go and see
The one I loved so dearly
Oh why God, can't it be?
But I am being just too selfish
And what I really know
Is that it is better there
And how I wish I could too.
I am not saying I want to die
But it wouldn't be so bad
Cause I wouldn't feel the pain
the 'Mother' I once had.

— Joanne

Sample Logs

The following sample logs from the first five sessions of a primary adolescent support group illustrate how helpful keeping a record can be. Keeping a short record allows leaders to track the progress or lack thereof of each counsellee and keep their stories straight. It is also helpful in planning for the next session.

Date: _____ Leaders: _____

The eight group members: Marilyn, Greg & Lisa (brother and sister), Gidget, Martha, Stephanie, Janis, and Jim.

Session 1, October 10:
Beginning – goals, information, comfort, confidentiality
Introduction – significant death

MARILYN – mother died of cancer – found it very difficult to talk – very close to mother – cremated – mother's ashes sent to Scotland – very lonely – father rarely at home because always working/drinking – Marilyn has close boyfriend – very close to boyfriend's mother – talks to her about the death, not to father.

G R E G – very angry – father out walking on shoulder of road – hit head on big pickup truck – driver drinking? – paramedics worked on father for 20 minutes – no time to say goodbye – funeral in Hamilton – lawsuit pending.

L I S A – too upset to talk – didn't want them to close casket – very close to father – passed on to Gidget.

G I D G E T – sleeping in station wagon on way to cottage – tire blew and car turned over – got out of car and asked if brother (Dave) was OK – no answer – both taken to hospital – brother died – Gidget had to remain in hospital – finally told brother died – could not attend funeral – very angry – would not speak to mother's boyfriend driving car for one year – she has become big problem at home – always argumentative – will not follow any discipline – skipping classes at school – poor grades – in danger of failing – using drugs?

M A R T H A – father died of cancer – under treatment for three years – recently started chemotherapy – lied to her about how sick he was – regrets she did not get along better with him – talked about how awful he looked before he died – down to 70 lbs – died at home – created problem – police came – was three hours before body removed – could not cry at funeral – laughed at funeral – mother angry with her – mother refuses to dispose of ashes, pictures, clothing, etc. – still very depressed and distressed.

S T E P H A N I E – father died in Nova Scotia – some kind of canoe accident – remembering phone call from police as they could not locate father's body – said very little after that.

J A N I S – was at home with father in rec. room – father went to light barbecue – it exploded – heard him scream – on fire – she could not help – tried to get neighbours to help – no one home – finally ambulance arrived – father to hospital – died two days later – very horrible – mother blames Janis for father's death.

J E F F – older brother Matt killed by hit-and-run driver – walking along side of bridge – remembers seeing him in casket –

mother very upset – closed casket for funeral – uncomfortable in group, expressing his feelings.

Session 2, October 17:
Feelings/Mandala
Goals – get members to add information re death

M A R I L Y N – quiet during this session – very worried – favourite aunt (sister of mother) has cancer – father will send her to California for visit – brought group a picture of her mother to show us – no one asked for picture – shared with group.

G R E G – very angry over father's death – should have jumped out of way – police have not laid any charges – believes driver was drinking – angry at mother who is not coping very well – rarely at home – has new job at drug store – also volunteering at hospital – little time for him or Lisa – both kids left to themselves – much sibling fighting at home.

L I S A – talked about funeral – mother was tipsy – also went hysterical during funeral – Graham hid in closet after funeral and cried – would not come out – mother also needs sleeping pills – lots of conflict at home between mother and kids.

G I D G E T – sick/absent.

M A R T H A – now says it was her grandfather who died, but grandfather was really her 'father because she never knew her biological father' – her biological parents? are in Europe (France) – mother is hospitalized as schizophrenic – her 'mother' here is really her mother's (biological) sister (eg., aunt) – Martha is angry because now her aunt/mother is dating her grandfather's younger brother, who never came to see him when he was ill – even the relatives in Europe did not seem to care or attend the funeral.

S T E P H A N I E – father was working on nuclear research in Nova Scotia – only came home every few months – went out canoeing on river – found canoe but not body – took several weeks to locate body – father finally shipped home – closed casket – was father really in there? – doesn't remember much about funeral – many people in house – lots of confusion – will be 'investigation' about his death – an aunt has sent mother newspaper clippings but she has not seen them – mother has hidden them away.

J A N I S – retold how father died – very terrible – large funeral – very respected in community – much anger at how slow ambulance was to respond – could not help father – mother was not home – father jumped in pool to try to save himself – terrible images of her burnt father.

J E F F – gave group more information – police finally caught driver through paint samples left on brother's body – had been stopped by police earlier for suspected drinking but police had to leave because of robbery call – lost licence – police feel brother died instantly – wants to go looking for driver.

All group members completed mandalas and each explained his/her mandala.

Leader's notes:
– Begin to talk about funeral itself.
– Remember Gidget missed this session.

Session 3: October 24:
Funeral/Wake
Transition stage

Group started.

G I D G E T – in hospital when brother died – told of funeral week after – very angry. She could not attend – also angry with doctors re treatment – has been to grave to see headstone – likes it – nice colour.

J E F F – does not remember much of funeral – closed coffin because of hit and run – many of his school friends came – played music which was recorded because brother was in rock group – used school pictures – mother very upset – had no use for service or the minister.

J A N I S – talked about funeral – very large – written up in paper – father well respected in community – closed casket – badly burned – brother pallbearer – mother seemed 'out of it' – big reception after – many people drunk – she was drinking with older sisters – mother very angry and blames her for father's death – she is suffering from flashbacks.

STEPHANIE – many problems returning body from Nova Scotia
– one month later memorial service – Stephanie read poem
she had written for her father – very beautiful – many friends
told stories about her father – wasn't sad – over 200 people –
beautiful reception at church – learned a lot about her father
because of his business connections.

GREG & LISA – big funeral in Burlington – open casket. Lisa
did not want to see father – didn't want them to lose casket –
was tipsy at funeral – slept with mother – had to be sedated at
funeral – Greg hid in the closet and cried by himself for hours
until uncle came and found him and tried to help him – had
terrible nightmares about funeral.

MARTHA – very angry at whole funeral process – 'friend' of
father showed up at funeral – never came to see her father
when he was ill – M. believes he has designs on her mother –
even the many relatives in Europe did not send a card/
flowers – whole funeral was one big party held at mother's
expense.

MARILYN – talked about funeral – mother Scottish, father not –
many of father's friends had been drinking – mother looked
'nice' – coffin was closed for public viewing – because mother
had cancer and was really thin – two of her aunts came from
Scotland – very pleased – they reminded her of her mother –
body was cremated so some of her ashes could be sent to
Scotland – mother's mother still alive but did not attend funeral – Marilyn's boyfriend has been a great support for her.

Leader's notes:
– Gave students telephone list to contact one another.
– Reminded students to bring pictures, keepsake, anything for
  session 4.

Session 4, October 31:
Remembering the deceased – pictures, good/bad memories
Suicide check

GIDGET – brought brother's high school pictures – always
thought he was a 'hero' on football team – his friends always
liked her – now no older brother to look out for her.

JEFF – seemed very depressed today – showed pictures again – angry with police – punching holes in wall at home – talked to school social worker re referral – mother not coping very well – older brother turning into hero.

JANIS – brought picture of dad sailing boat – many happy memories – having very difficult time – experiencing flashbacks of seeing her father burning – having 'no skin' – felt helpless – no car to take father to hospital – tried to get neighbours to assist – still 'fears' hospitals – felt doctors let her down – sometimes wishes she had died and not father – many conflicts at home – talked to school psychologist re Janis.

STEPHANIE – proudly showed picture of father in Algonquin Park canoeing with friends – also brought a trophy he had won – has decided to start swimming (training) again and swims on school team – wants to do well in school – perhaps win swimming scholarship so father will be proud of her – showed family portrait and then began to talk.

GREG & LISA – mother suing driver of truck – large lawsuit going on – Lisa misses her father, who helped her every night with her math – Lisa fighting with mother – mother worried about finances – both kids feel they cannot grieve at home because this upsets mother – Lisa having great deal of difficulty in school (math).

MARILYN – found showing picture of mother very difficult – was very close to her mother – did not see much of her father – had only many positive memories of mother – shopping at Square One – watching TV together – having dinner together – is now very close to her boyfriend's mother and feels she can talk to her.

MARTHA – told the group her story – her mother here is really mother's sister (aunt) – real mother lives in France and is in mental hospital – her father (unknown) here is her grandfather, but the only father she has ever known – although very old, loved her as a father – great support – took her everywhere and did everything with her – too embarrassed to tell her friends he was her grandfather – although he was much 'older' than her peers' fathers.

Leader's notes:
- Who has used their telephone list?
- Social work/permission forms, etc. – Jeff, Janis.
- Psychology.

Session 5, November 5:
Problem-solving
How death has changed your life – problems students may face
after death

GREG & LISA – lots of problems at home – mother finding it
very difficult to cope – using tranquillizers – goes to bed early
– does not spend much time with them – few meals – trying to
get grandmother from Burlington to stay in house to help but
lost husband last year – finding it difficult herself to cope –
Greg now having lots of conflicts with mother – feels she should
listen to him (man of the house).

JANIS – much difficulty at home – mother blames her for
father's death – constantly fighting with older brother (physical) – was on national team for diving – wants to quit – father
was her coach – much acting out – will not respect curfew –
mother thinking about joining tough love – have taken away
her house key – driving mother's car without permission.

JEFF – mother now thinks brother could do no wrong – room is
'special place' – extra special place in house – mother has
added extra pictures – cards from funeral – high school di-
ploma – Jeff skipping school – not doing assignments – in
serious danger of failing all credits – mother wants him to
work hard – cannot concentrate – only attends art class.

STEPHANIE – finding it difficult to get to swim practice – father
used to take her – mother working long hours in Toronto –
keeping her marks up so she can get car – wants to go to U.S.
on swimming scholarship.

GIDGET – feeling somewhat better – still in physio – frightened
about upcoming holiday – going to drive to South Carolina –
finds it hard to get in car – angry at mother's boyfriend Fred
who was driving car – mother should get rid of him – not doing

very well in school – absent great deal because of physio – teachers becoming angry because of so many missed periods.

M A R I L Y N – very lonely – father is always working or going to the pub on the way home from work or after – only child – her grades are not good and she has no one who is interested in her progress – trying to gain acceptance in program at CAAT (Community College) – will have counsellor (Jane) write reference letter for her.

M A R T H A – very angry at aunt (mother) who is now dating new man who showed up at funeral – suddenly aunt is wearing much 'younger' clothes and acting like a teenager – at school Martha is working very hard because she wants her aunt to send her to France to see her real mother who is schizophrenic, and she only has a picture of her as a younger girl – her relatives in France have agreed to put her up for the summer and find her a job – if she does well at school – very bright student and gifted in languages.

Finally, counsellors may wish to make use of the sample permission and teacher notification forms in use at Lorne Park Secondary School. These are given in detail on pages 53 and 54.

Sample Forms

The following permission form is given to students during their intake interview. It is to be signed, then returned to the school.

Sample Permission Form for Adolescents under 16

(date)

TO:
RE: GROUP COUNSELLING (Coping with Grief)

Your young person has been asked to participate in Group Counselling sessions. Acceptance is voluntary on the student's part and the sessions will probably last for three months (ten sessions). The Group will meet once a week from 2:00 p.m. to 3:00 p.m.

We hope it will be an opportunity for students to meet with other members of the Group and discuss topics of mutual interest or concern. As group leaders, we will be involved in every group meeting.

If you should require any further information, please feel free to call us at the school.

If you agree to your child taking part in these sessions, please sign below and have your child return this letter to the Counselling Office.

Yours sincerely,

LORNE PARK SECONDARY SCHOOL
Grant W. Baxter – Head, Counselling Services
Wendy Stuart, RN – School Nurse

_____

Parent's Signature

This form is sent to the bereaved student's teachers, to advise them of the student's participation in the group.

Sample Teacher Notification Form

LORNE PARK SECONDARY SCHOOL
Counselling Services

TO: The teachers of   _____
         Home Group: _____
                Period: A _____
                          B _____
                          C _____
                          D _____

_____ will be involved with group counselling (Coping with Grief and Bereavement Counselling) sessions which meet every Wednesday at 2:00 p.m. – 3:00 p.m. for one hour. There will be approximately ten sessions.

If you wish any further information, please ask either Wendy Stuart or myself.
    Thank you for your co-operation in this matter.

Yours sincerely,
Grant Baxter
Wendy Stuart

3. *Common Problems*

This chapter illustrates some of the problems faced by bereaved adolescents – problems that have become clearly observable as groups have progressed.

Health

Health and physical well-being are affected by bereavement, and some common complaints are disturbed sleeping and eating patterns (not eating, eating too much, and waking up several times a night). Bereaved adolescents sometimes will believe they are suffering from the same disease that killed their loved one, and they can experience and 'feel the pain' of the deceased. They also often suffer from headaches and general malaise, and want to miss school and stay at home to recover.

Hallucinations/Imagery

Hallucinations occur most often at night. These can assume an olfactory form, such as experiencing the smell of earth or the perfume of flowers; they can also be auditory, such as hearing a loved one's car in the driveway or the car door slam; or they can be visual, such as waking to see the deceased standing in the room. Such sightings can be positive, such as the deceased reassuring the adolescent that he or she is now in a 'better place.' But, more often, 'visions' such as these are disturbing, and the adolescent will need to get out of bed, turn on the light, look at a pleasant picture of the deceased, and then try to impose the good picture over the bad. Hallucinations also occur during waking hours, though less frequently. At these times adolescents will think they see the deceased, say, in a crowd walking through a mall, when it is actually someone of the same physical size and appearance who resembles the deceased. At these times, adolescents have been known to cry out and perhaps touch or stare at the stranger.

Suicide

Some time after a death, some students have considered suicide. For some it is because their pain and despair are unbearable. For others, the motivating force is the desire to join the lost loved one. In any case, group leaders must always ask, quite openly, 'Who has considered suicide?' and follow with a full discussion of what the adolescent had in mind – the proposed method, time, place, etc. Most students are not high risks for suicide, but if leaders have any doubts, they must refer such students to additional therapy with a professional specializing in bereavement counselling (see Session 4, p. 49).

In some settings, such as school boards, there may be particular guidelines or contracts for counsellors to follow. But *do not think the condition will go away, or the adolescent will feel better tomorrow.* His or her parents may also need to be contacted in order to arrange an appropriate intervention. Emergency departments at local hospitals and family physicians can also be very helpful.

Difficulties at Home

In spite of the blurring of gender differences in our society, it is not unusual for surviving parents to assign to adolescents the traditional parenting roles. Males are expected to do yard work, snow shovelling, garbage disposal, minor house repairs, etc., and females are expected to look after younger children, do laundry, cook, etc. Fulfilling these roles often results in conflict with the school as both become full-time, competing jobs.

This introduction of new duties and more restrictive rules is difficult for adolescents, as is the opposite case: no rules at all.

Or perhaps the surviving parent becomes absent emotionally and ceases to enforce the old rules, or must work extended hours outside the home. Another common problem is the introduction of a new partner, and possibly his or her children, too quickly after a death. If the surviving parent has met the partner before the death, the bereaved adolescent can become even more confused and angry. Suddenly there could be new stepsisters or stepbrothers invading the space of the surviving adolescent(s), creating personality clashes between the old and new families. The problems experienced by newly blended families following a death are often the most traumatic for young people. They cannot accept the replacement parents under any circumstances, and since they are excluded from the decision-making, bitter conflicts often result over discipline, different roles within the 'family' and injured feelings.

Visiting Hospital

Young people are usually healthy. They usually have not been exposed a great deal to elderly or ill people; thus, visiting the hospital can be a traumatic experience and they may only stay for a short while or won't go at all. Other patients' illnesses and treatment procedures (tubes, respirators) may also frighten them, or, when visiting their own parent or sibling, they may feel uncomfortable in the presence of a person who, because of drugs or other treatments, is unable to communicate. Often, adolescents do not have transportation, or parents will want them in school. In some families, adolescents are not encouraged to visit the hospital, even when they wish to. They may want to spend all their time at the bedside; and their parents may be concerned that they keep up their grades, which may not be possible, with or without the time lost. However, this kind of discouragement can create a no-win situation, making bereaved adolescents feel torn and guilty. They need to be reassured and given the opportunity to choose. The schoolwork can be attended to later; a parent/sibling/friend/classmate is seriously ill now. However, to pass the school year, another semester may be needed.

Relocation

Sometimes the death of a parent means making a move to a new home, coupled with a reduction of finances and the loss of friends, school, neighbours and pets. Adolescents worry about family finances, but often won't ask about them for fear of bad news – that they won't be able, now, to continue their education, for example. Or they may not want to bother the surviving parent with such 'mundane' subjects as money, and will instead retreat into themselves or perhaps play the martyr role.

Post-Secondary Education

Students who have suffered a bereavement just prior to undertaking post-secondary education are often highly at risk to fail their first year. Many students can feel overwhelmed with campus life, with its more difficult scholastic standards, assignments, and reading materials, as well as its emotional issues: classmates, roommates, friends, etc. Group leaders have found that it is helpful if bereaved students reduce their academic course load by 50 per cent, postpone their post-secondary education for a year, or complete an extension program as an alternative. Such a decision could avoid a young person's feeling that he or she has not only lost a parent, but is a failure at academics as well. Most colleges and universities today are understanding of the problems of bereaved students, and will work with them to find suitable solutions. Post-secondary education is an expensive investment for any student, and these students do not want to add another year, thus making it even more costly.

Student Check List

The following points are important concerns bereaved group participants have identified following the death of a parent, sibling, close friend, etc. The list will be most useful to parents, relatives, and friends of grieving adolescents, who will need 'someone to listen' and understand.

- Not wanting to go out and leave surviving parent alone
- Disliking 'weird' things people say and do at funerals
- Having dreams, hallucinations
- Being called the dead sibling's name
- Taking telephone calls for the dead person
- Anniversaries of the death, Christmas, birthdays, etc.
- Inability to concentrate at times
- Not wanting others to forget the person who has died
- Hero worship of the dead sibling
- Inability to talk with parents or parent about the death because of emotions
- Not knowing all the facts surrounding the death; angry over secrets kept
- Parent bringing home male or female friend; resenting surviving parent trying to replace lost parent
- Disliking new, strict rules (overprotection), or the opposite (being left to fend for themselves)
- Feeling guilty (suicidal) – should have noticed and helped
- Wishing would have spent more time with a dying parent
- Not believing the body buried; thinking someone simply removed the body and took it away in the hearse
- Needing to see the body to believe the person has died (see When Bodies Cannot Be Recovered, p. 15)
- Not wanting pity; rather, wanting recognition
- Not liking idea of a party or wake after the funeral
- Having difficulty when surviving parent remarries
- Unable to go to hospital to see a parent at the end
- Having to endure many significant losses after the death: a change of school, a move, the loss of a pet/friends/relatives
- Feeling angry that a parent or sibling has died and left them; being unable to understand the anger
- Feeling shame if death is by suicide; giving others a different reason for the death
- Having a desperate need to talk and '*have someone listen*'

4. Case Studies: Grieving Special Losses

The following case studies illustrate some of the common themes/ problems experienced by grieving adolescents.

Survival Myth or Hero Worship Syndrome

The mother of a student accidentally killed coming home from school could not come to terms with her grief. Her son had become a hero in her eyes. Three years after his death, everything in his room was exactly the same as the day he died; no one could touch anything in the room or even enter it without the mother's permission. She also slept in her son's bed. She had forgotten that her son had been simply a normal, fourteen-year-old student. His two older brothers could not relate to their mother in her grief, the parents quarrelled continually, and the son's death finally resulted in marital breakdown, which in turn deprived the brothers of their mother's care.

Inhibited Grief

Often, group members will give example of 'inhibited' grief as it is experienced with their fathers. Because many men still feel society expects them not to show emotion, to 'be tough,' they find it difficult to show their grief, especially in front of their teenagers. As a result, men who have lost a spouse will often immerse themselves in work, a response sometimes interpreted by adolescents as a lack of love for their mother. Some men also find a substitute for their deceased spouse too quickly – immediately following the death, and sometimes before the death if it has followed a lengthy terminal illness.

States of Family Renewal/Blended Families

Griefwork takes a long time to accomplish. Often, surviving parents do not allow enough time for this process to work, and the results can be disastrous. Tim's mother remarried one month after the terrible accidental death of her husband following an oil drum explosion. Tim loved his father and was angry at his mother, whom he felt should still be grieving for his father. Tim also resented his new stepfather, and because he was the oldest in the family he was expected to carry more responsibility and set an example for his younger brothers and sisters. His stepfather was not a warm, loving person like his father, but a perfectionist and a workaholic. Tim's anger towards his stepfather and anger towards his mother resulted in terrible family disputes that eventually broke up the family.

Suicide: Anger, Sense of Abandonment, Acceptance

Students who have lost a parent, sibling, close relation, or friend through suicide demand much more attention from the group. They will often tell their stories many times over, and will exhibit much more anger and guilt towards the suicide victim than will other members of the group. This was the story of Vee.

A ward of the Children's Aid Society, Vee had many emotional problems and had been living away from her family off and on for many years. While Vee was living at a group home, her mother committed suicide. The court ordered that she not be told the cause of death, but she was allowed to go to the funeral and to the cemetery. It was also very difficult to get permission for her to join the group, but persistence paid off and she eventually was allowed to join. The first session was very difficult for her and she tried to leave, but after a quiet time outside she returned and related how her mother had overdosed on drugs. Though she was understanding of the fact that her mother had been depressed, Vee was very angry because her mother had been a nurse and she felt her mother should have known better. She was also very angry at the silence imposed by the CAS, and its reluctance to give her the facts surrounding her mother's death.

Once the group sessions were over Vee told the authorities that she knew the cause of her mother's death and that her father blamed her for it; that he told her she was sent to a group home because she caused so many problems for her mother over the years that they could not keep her at home. After several group sessions Vee came to feel that her father was a little late with his accusations and she was able to tell him that her mother was responsible for her own actions. The group had given her that strength. When she first came into the group, she swore regularly and was very sloppy in her appearance. After three to four weeks the swearing stopped, the attention-getting ceased, and she dressed more neatly. She also made friends with the others in the group, and in the end it was hard to believe she was the same person. She had become quite popular with her peers and was also doing better in school.

When dealing with suicides group leaders have observed that patterns are different than those resulting from 'more regular' deaths, or those where families have had an opportunity to deal with some of their grief beforehand.

Kim, a grade ten student who lost her older sister through suicide, had waited until group sessions began before releasing her feelings surrounding the death of her sister. Kim's sister had been a very clever senior student, an Ontario Scholar. In high school she had been an extremely popular young person, an outstanding athlete, cheerleader, member of the student council – a girl who had obtained both her athletic and academic letters. She had then gone on to university, but soon dropped out. She returned the next year, but dropped out again, because, being a perfectionist she had set such high goals for herself she found them impossible to obtain. At the time of her death she had been hospitalized as a potential suicide risk and was under psychiatric care. Unfortunately, as is sometimes the case, just as she appeared to be on the road to recovery she hanged herself in the basement of the family home.

In the group, Kim showed many signs of both anger and love. She continually questioned why her sister had done this to her and to her family. In questioning the group, she often addressed her sister directly: 'I loved you, I admired you. You were the perfect sister. Why did you do this to us? You were the successful one, the beautiful one, the intelligent one. You had everything going for you. How do I tell people what has happened to my sister?' One frequent experience that was particularly upsetting to Kim was being called by her dead sister's name. However, by the end of the group she was better able to accept her sister's death, and her anger began to diminish. She then felt she was ready for further therapy outside the group.

Taking on Disease/Illness

John, who still refused to join the group two years after the death of his mother, was still full of anger and had punched many holes in his bedroom walls to prove it. An attempt was made to get him into outside counselling, but these efforts were not successful. John had experienced some symptoms of abdominal distress, and he felt sure he had cancer, just like his mother. He had extensive tests and was given a clean bill of health, but didn't believe the doctors. John was always sick and missed a great deal of school. The end result was failing grades, and he eventually dropped out. At home, away from their peers, such students can become depressed very quickly and sometimes become suicidal. Unfortunately, in the end John became a 'street kid' on the streets of Toronto.

Unexplained or Sudden Death

Beverly was asked to join the group although her parents had been dead for over six years. Her mother had left the home one day after saying goodbye, and was last seen driving away. It wasn't until one year later that the police found her murdered remains seventy-five miles away, behind an abandoned building. Her father had become an alcoholic, and Beverly was convinced he had committed suicide, one year later, with a mix of pills and 'booze.' She had never been told details of either death, she did not attend either funeral, nor had she seen either grave. The youngest in the family, she had lived in turn with her older sisters. She resented the fact that no one would tell her the truth, and group members encouraged her to find out what happened on her own. She remembered each death vividly: she was alone, tried unsuccessfully to awaken her father, and eventually ran out of the house to use the telephone in the plaza down the street. She told the same story three times in great detail, never changing a word. She was encouraged to seek outside help, and she eventually saw a psychiatrist. She had a lot of difficulty in school and it was hoped that outside counselling would help. After several years of counselling, she finally graduated from high school, and has been able to lead a productive and happy life.

In another example of a sudden death situation, a plane crash took the life of a pilot, the father of two adolescent girls, Donna and Dawn. The investigation that followed was slow and piecemeal, and finally concluded that the crash was caused by pilot error. The distress caused by the lengthy investigation – court dates, insurance investigations, and publicity – delayed the girls' normal grief reactions. As well, when an accident resulting in death is caused by the deceased, there is much anger and guilt which the survivors must work through before grieving can begin to take place. Adolescents who have experienced this kind of death certainly can benefit from being part of the group, but they will sometimes require extra individual counselling from co-leaders. It may also be necessary to refer them for outside therapy.

Humour

Sometimes, adolescents tell 'funny stories' in the group, which do 'lighten up' one's day. Here is a typical story about disposing of ashes. Debbie, accompanied by her two sisters and older brother, decided it would be fitting to dispose of their father's ashes on the golf course where he played at least twice a week before he died of cancer. While the mother agreed to this, she did not wish to take part. It was dark and raining when they went out onto the course. Feeling nervous, they laughed a little, but eventually settled down and chose a spot where the cremated remains would be scattered. They said a prayer, scattered the ashes, and then set off to return by elevator to the clubhouse. Unfortunately, the elevator was not working, and they ended up having to climb a muddy hill. Slipping, sliding, and laughing, they felt that their father's spirit was there with them, laughing as well. They said they would never forget it. Debbie shared this story so freely with the group that one boy was encouraged to talk about the cremated remains of his mother, which were at home on the mantelpiece in an urn. He said he felt uncomfortable that they were there, but that his father could not decide what to do with them. Group members said they shared his feelings. They also gave him some suggestions for disposing of them. It is helpful for group leaders to remember that when dealing with adolescents a little humour never hurt anyone, and besides, it can result in some excellent problem-solving in the group.

Hallucinations, Dreams, Flashbacks

It is very common for students to report hallucinations in connection with the deceased, and to see them in dreams. Students often report seeing the deceased walking in a crowd in a shopping centre or hearing them arrive at the house (for example, the sound of the family car coming into the driveway or garage). They often report seeing the deceased standing at the foot of the bed or at the top of the stairs. Some students did not seem overly upset or frightened by these hallucinations but, rather, reported feeling comforted by them. However, some students did find the experience upsetting.

Delayed Grief

Cindy came into the nurse's office in great distress. A long time passed before she could settle down to talk, but when she did it was very meaningful. She had been reading a story in class about a young man with a terminal illness who had killed himself, and she soon recognized that the young man in the story was a favourite cousin who had died six years previously. She had been only ten years old at the time, and had not been allowed to go to the funeral; as a result, she had never grieved for him. After all those years it all came pouring out.

Grieving Timetables

Many siblings report that they receive very little support from their parents during the grieving process. The parents are busy doing their own grieving, or not grieving at all, and when the children want to talk about the dead parent, often the surviving parent becomes too emotional to talk about him or her. If the surviving parent shows too much grief, adolescents may become frightened, then not mention it again for fear of upsetting the parent. Communication around the death then becomes very difficult for everyone.

Death of Siblings

Sally, a member of the group whose twelve-year-old sister had been ill, was told by her parents not to tell her sister the medical diagnosis. It was terrible for Sally not to be able to answer her sister's questions. When Sally's sister came home to die the problem became worse, until one day Sally asked her sister for a book to read. Her sister threw a book at her. It was called *A Summer to Die*. She said, 'Read this ... it's just like our family.' The story was about a teenager who dies of leukaemia. After reading the book the sisters never spoke about it, or about the sister's illness, but they got along better once they both knew. Sally never told her parents about this event. It was their own secret.

The death of a child, either by disease, accident, suicide, or murder is a horrific event for any family to experience, with its pain, guilt, its many unanswered questions, its unfulfilled dreams. And if the death is unexplained there is the waiting for police and coroner's reports, the delays of the court system, the lack of justice in the justice system, the media, the reactions of friends. The list goes on and on.

In the case of Brent, killed by a drunk driver, the surviving sisters often blamed themselves for their brother's death: 'If only he had left three minutes earlier. Why did he take the short cut? He had been warned a thousand times to ride his bike on the sidewalk. Why couldn't one of us have died instead of him? He had his whole life to live. He was so young. Brent was our only brother. He was such a good boy, an outstanding student, good athlete,' and so on. Such a death places tremendous strain on everyone, even on a good marriage. It is a fact that approximately 50 per cent of marriages fail after the death of a child. In this case the older siblings and the father seemed to be grieving normally, but the mother was showing abnormal grief patterns. The two older girls had to account to her for every minute: Where were they going? With whom? How? They couldn't drive for fear of another accident. Brent was killed by a young offender who merely received a fine and a suspended sentence, a seeming lack of justice that complicated the grieving process. However, in this case, once all this was finally settled, the family members began to grieve in earnest, and the surviving sisters went on to lead successful lives.

Abortion

This topic is included because it illustrates another type of loss, though most bereavement groups do not include students who have had an abortion. However, students contemplating abortion, or who have had an abortion, do grieve.

There are many issues surrounding this decision. At times, it is not their decision but their parents'. They are in shock, feel sad and lonely, and have many concerns. They will give reasons why they are unable to have the child. Still, according to Corr and McNeil, in their book *Adolescence and Death*, most would, if the time was right, they were older, or had support, continue the pregnancy. They grieve the loss of the child, and many carry this loss their whole lives. Many often unconsciously forget to take the pill or don't use effective birth control, wanting to be pregnant, to have someone of their own to love, someone who will love them. Students having home and personal difficulties are often the ones who find themselves pregnant, and then realize they are unable to cope with yet another problem.

As Corr and McNeil note, it is important for all (counsellors, family, friends) supporting these young women to understand that a whole gamut of feelings will follow at different times, from relief to guilt and regret. It is so important to listen and not judge, to be supportive, to reassure them that all these feelings are normal. Young men will have these feelings as well, but most don't verbalize them.

One school nurse sees at least three to four students a year who are having trouble dealing with their feelings after an abortion – especially if they didn't have a choice in the matter. 'It is a highly visible moral and social issue which may create the need for death-related counselling.'[1] The students are angry, and because it is a secret they cannot reveal, believe no one appreciates how they feel. One young woman saw the nurse before and after an abortion and also received some outside counselling. She sought help on her own, with no family members involved. Her parents did not suspect anything, and thought that all was well. However, when her grandfather died a few months later she completely fell apart and signed herself into hospital for therapy.

Another student, whose father is a doctor, was forced into having an abortion, and was not allowed to see the young man who fathered the child. She tried to cope, but eventually ran away and talked about suicide. The parents arranged for professional help but the student did not like the doctor, a friend of her father's, though she did promise to give him a second chance. The school nurse suggested she decide beforehand what she was going to say about the abortion, and to ask the questions that needed answers. The student concluded that the doctor was nicer than she thought, and reported that he was glad she came prepared with questions. She said she felt much better, and planned to continue to see him, reassured that even though he was her father's friend, that the sessions would be held in confidence.

---

1 Corr and McNeil, *Adolescence and Death*, 217.

5. Ways Schools and Parents Can Assist

One does not have to be a professional counsellor to help bereaved adolescents. Schools can help by reaching out to the communities they serve and being prepared to help when required. There is no substitute for the caring support of a young person's family members, but neither is there a substitute for the support of warm, sympathetic individuals in our schools, who try to 'be there' for the grieving teenager.

How Teachers Can Help

DO:

- Let the student know you are aware of the death in his or her family, or of a friend.
- Let the student know that you understand how painful or difficult life is for him or her right now.
- Visit the funeral home or attend the funeral, and sign the guest book so that the student will know you were there.
- Send a card or note addressed to the student rather than to the family.
- Tell the student you are there to provide extra help with his or her studies, assignments, and courses; and then follow through.
- Set specific times to meet with the student, who may be floundering academically.
- Be prepared to let the student talk, not only about academic problems, but also about the death, his or her feelings, and any problems at home.

- Share your own experiences of the death of a loved one with the student if you have had such an experience.
- Be aware of the changed family structure and the resulting problems caused by a death in the family, and tell the student you are aware of these additional stresses.
- Recognize that physical symptoms such as insomnia, loss of appetite, headaches, and stomach-aches are a normal part of grief, and can affect both the quantity and quality of a student's work.
- If you are a counsellor, be knowledgeable concerning the available community resources, and pass the appropriate information along to the student.
- Offer to inform other classmates, friends, and teachers about the bereavement.

DON'T:

- Ignore the death.
- Say 'It takes time.'
  - 'Time heals.'
  - 'Try to get back to normal.'
  - 'It's time to pull up your socks and get on with life.'
  - 'The show must go on.'
  - 'Life is for the living.'
- Expect the student to be unchanged by the death.
- Expect the student to behave and perform academically as before.
- Lay your goals or expectations on the student by saying:
  - 'You'll lose marks.'
  - 'You won't graduate.'
  - 'You'll fail your exam.'
- Single the student out in front of others for missed classes, incomplete assignments, or lack of concentration.
- Be sarcastic or intolerant of the student's appearance or behaviour.
- Be judgmental or inflexible.
- Allow other students in the class to put down or make fun of the grieving student.

- Do or say anything to the student that you would not want done or said to you under the same circumstances.

How Parents Can Help

- Inform the educational institution of the death so that teaching staff and counsellors will be aware; also try to keep the institution informed of any ongoing problems.
- Communication is the key. Try to tell the truth to adolescents about the events surrounding the death or illness; give young people as much detail as possible; try not to feel that you must protect teenagers from the truth.
- If an adolescent has never attended a funeral before, try to explain what will happen (ritual) and what they will see. Adolescents find viewing the body very difficult, and can be offended as well by aspects of the ritual: for example, when people appear happy if alcohol has been served at the following reception or wake.
- Remember that adolescents often 'act out' to mask anger and depression because they find it difficult to express grief in appropriate ways. Remember that they are really asking for help and recognition.
- Remember that griefwork is often complicated by adolescents' physical/emotional developmental stages, such as hormonal changes and seeking independence from their families.
- Try to give ongoing emotional and physical support.
- Be prepared to accept less achievement at school, though sometimes teenagers will attempt to cope by becoming overly involved with their schoolwork and/or their jobs.
- Try to keep a balance at home. For example, try not to overprotect, and yet be prepared to set limits on unacceptable behaviour and stick to it.
- Try to retain continuity. For example, remain in the same residence/school if possible. This allows a continuation of life as it was before. This way, old friendships and a sense of security can be maintained.
- Try to prepare one meal a day so that the family can be together; this allows communication and keeps up a routine.

- If possible, try to talk about the future: what is likely to happen regarding finances and further education, and, should the surviving parent die, who would be responsible for the adolescent. Discussions like this can be difficult, but they do help decrease the adolescent's anxiety.
- Try to delay serious involvement with the opposite sex; it just complicates the grieving process.
- Talk over how you would like to disperse the deceased's possessions, and ask your adolescent for help in carrying out this task. There may be things he or she treasures and would like to keep.
- Talk about how you are feeling and encourage other family members to do so, especially when special occasions arise such as an anniversary of the death, Christmas, or birthdays. Make special plans together.
- Remember that each person grieves differently, depending on such factors as one's relationship with the deceased or how the death occurred.
- Try not to use adolescents as your bereavement support group. Remember, it is a sign of strength to be able to seek professional help, for example, from grief therapists, social workers, clergy, and organizations such as Bereaved Families of Ontario/ SADD, Theos, and Peel Family Services.
- Recognize that the death has changed the adolescent.
- Listen and use your common sense – it is usually correct.

Effective Methods of Coping[1]

The verb 'to cope' means to struggle or contend, especially on even terms or with a degree of success. How do bereaved families cope? Some ideas:
- Have family meetings regularly. Share how each member of the family is *really* doing.

---

1 From the Benjamin Institute for Community Education and Referral, Toronto. Reprinted with permission.

- Write down and share an assessment of your personal needs.
- Find out about the cognitive level of understanding of surviving members and deal with them accordingly.
- Cry, or let others do so. Get your feelings out.
- Face life just one day at a time.
- Listen to your own common sense and avoid the 'shoulds' of others.
- Take care of yourself first.
- Schedule pleasurable activities.
- Get out of the house.
- Ask someone to accompany you on difficult outings.
- Resume activities gradually. Give yourself a push as you feel able. You must work to overcome inertia. Keep busy, but *don't overdo it.*
- Exercise regularly and get plenty of fresh air.
- Eat nutritiously.
- Honour the memory of the deceased by making a positive decision to work through grief. Look for reasons to go on.
- Do your griefwork. Experience each painful reaction.
- Be aware that drugs and alcohol can delay and decelerate the grief process.
- Draw strength from every possible source.
- Use and maintain support systems such as family, friends, and support groups.
- Read about the grief process, various near-death experiences, and after-life beliefs.
- Keep a journal.
- Use relaxation techniques such as yoga, meditation, self-hypnosis, and listening to relaxation tapes or music.
- Write a letter to your deceased family member and say all the things you wish you could say in person.
- Write down irrational feelings of guilt and then throw them away.
- Accept death as a part of life.
- Work at redefining your beliefs.
- Express your feelings to other people and tell them what you need.

- Seek professional help if you get stuck.
- Don't be ashamed to ask for help.
- Educate others about grief.
- As you are able, force yourself to think about and do things for other people.
- Plan ahead for difficult days such as holidays and the anniversary of the death and consider making small changes in the way you celebrate these days.
- Sort through and/or give away some of the belongings of the deceased only when you are ready to do so.
- Carefully choose meaningful items that belonged to your loved one to give as mementos to special people, but be sure to keep those items that are important to you.
- Avoid rash decisions such as moving, divorce, changing jobs, or giving away all your loved one's possessions.
- Try to relive some of the good memories.
- Allow those close to you to grieve in their own manner and according to their own timetable.
- Grieve with your family but avoid overwhelming each other.
- Try talking with a trusted relative or friend.
- When you feel a need to fall apart, let yourself go.
- Give yourself permission to laugh.

When a Parent or Sibling Is Terminally Ill

The following are ways in which a school can support an adolescent who has a terminally ill parent or sibling.

- The counselling department, school nurse, or community health nurse should, within the limits of confidentiality, inform the student's teachers and make them aware of the situation.
- Teachers should be aware that students with terminally ill parents/siblings will not be able to concentrate and will appear tired from worry and/or from visiting or living with the patient. Often, the parent or sibling is dying at home, with all the problems that creates. Patience is required.

- During this period, be aware that students do not eat properly, get enough sleep, or look after themselves physically. As a result, they tend not to study or do homework, which teachers find frustrating. It is normal behaviour at this time, and the adolescent needs understanding.
- The school can arrange for peer counselling if there is a student who has undergone a similar experience and who could act as a 'buddy' for the adolescent.
- Teachers might encourage the student to try to communicate at home in order to establish a link between the school and the home. This might also encourage dialogue at home between the parent and adolescent.
- Teachers should remember that not all siblings will react the same way within the family; some adolescents will accept the support of the school and others will reject its attempts at support.
- If possible, the school can reassure a parent that their child will receive continuing counselling after the death or at least the support of a counsellor within a bereavement support group. This reassurance is often very comforting to the parent. He or she may not have been aware that such help from the school was possible.
- If a student is going on to a post-secondary institution, the school should inform the institution so that the terminal illness is taken into consideration during the admission process.

It has often been observed that if communication is possible before a death occurs, adolescents are left with much less guilt and anger to deal with after the death. If they are lucky, they may even have had time to discuss future hopes and plans, and to say goodbye.

When a Teacher Dies

It is most helpful if students can be told the true circumstances surrounding the death of a teacher. If possible, classes should be informed by a sympathetic teacher, and students should be given time to express their feelings. If they feel grief, students need an opportunity to talk about their relationship with the teacher. Such talk will not, as some believe, make things worse, but in the end will make things better.

At the end of the day, a school-wide announcement should be made, giving the date, time, and place of the funeral or memorial service. Maps might be provided, as well, so that interested staff and students may attend the service, and the school flag could be lowered as a sign of respect. (See Planning a Memorial Service, p. 79.)

When a Student Dies

It is very important that the school *immediately* acknowledge the death (preferably a teacher in each classroom). Again, time in the classroom should be allowed for students to express their feelings. Opportunities should also be provided for students to come together in a quiet place to share stories, memories, and feelings about the deceased. For example, following the tragic death of a student who was killed by a drunk driver, approximately thirty students, including friends and siblings, came together over the lunch hour to talk and to review the life of the deceased. The group also included counsellors and the local youth minister. Doing this during the school day formally recognized the death. Having the students in school, even though they were not attending classes, kept them safe. (Keeping students in school also provides an opportunity to form a group for the 'survivors.' Such groups meet for another two to five sessions, depending on the needs of the members.) It also gave permission for friends to be involved, in order to help themselves and to give support to surviving siblings in the school. In this case, the siblings were part of this group. The friends just arrived, knowing the school would support them. The group discussed anger over the circumstances of the death and shared honest feelings about the deceased that helped give perspective to the individual's life. Some of the adolescents cried, some were in shock, and some contributed stories concerning the deceased.

For the adolescents who were afraid of funerals or disliked them the group provided an opportunity to talk about these feelings and to learn what to expect. For example, they learned that funerals are often helpful, that they give friends and family an opportunity to say goodbye. Group members were also encouraged to write poems and share photographs, which reminded them that each person is an individual with a unique perspective on death and how it will effect him or her, that it is quite normal to be sad, that we all show sadness differently: some with tears, some with anger and/or lack of control. The students felt that allowing them to do this helped them accept the death. After about an hour, when they had finished sharing their thoughts, they disbanded. Individual counselling was then done when necessary.

When There Is Life-Threatening Illness

It would be ideal if the school could be made aware of the fact that an adolescent student has a family member who is experiencing a life-threatening illness. This would enable staff at the school to provide the necessary support and understanding. However, this is often very difficult for parents as well as the hospital staff, as terminal illness is often viewed as a personal family tragedy and families sometimes do not want to involve outside agencies. Often, families will not give the hospital permission to inform the school, even if the hospital is aware that there are siblings in the family. Adolescents also may be reluctant to visit a dying parent or sibling. Hospital and social workers usually work with a dying parent (father or mother) but often find it difficult to involve the children.

Parents are often unaware of how the impending death is affecting their adolescents. This lack of awareness, coupled with the fact that neither parent really expects anyone to die (even if they have been informed that this may happen), often results in social workers being denied permission to speak to involved adolescents. Often, a communication gap develops without the parent realizing what is happening because he/she is fully occupied with visiting the dying spouse or family member, trying to keep a job, doing household chores, and generally trying to hold the family together. The adolescents are also very busy, attending school, seeing friends, possibly working part-time, or participating in sports.

Social workers also do not want to upset a parent who is already looking after everything, and as a result, they often do not know the extent of the illness or are not told the truth.

Still, with encouragement and support, adolescents will visit the hospital, and floor nurses or social workers will try to help if they are informed of the pending visit beforehand. Adolescents are often afraid that there will be a crisis and he or she won't know what to do. Again, with the support of family or hospital personnel, adolescents should be encouraged to go with the ill parent or sibling for their chemotherapy or radiation treatments, in order to see the situation for themselves. Though it is hard on them, it is better that they be informed as much as possible, even if the experience leads to questions that no one has answers for: 'Why my family?' or 'Why did God do this?'

The Principal's Letter

Parents appreciate a letter of condolence from the school, written by the principal. As adolescents spend a great deal of their time at school and are often heavily involved in extracurricular activities, it is only fitting that they receive some acknowledgment. Though a difficult task for any administrator, it is an important one.

The School Yearbook

If asked, parents also appreciate the school's remembering their son or daughter in the In Memoriam section of the school yearbook. Parents will often contribute pictures, classmates' poetry, etc. A copy of the yearbook can then be presented to the parents by a favourite teacher, or perhaps by the deceased's best friend. The occasion, although sad, links the school and home, and can become, again, a time for sharing memories.

Planning a Memorial Service

In the summer of 1987 three Lorne Park students were killed in separate motor vehicle accidents. Because many students and staff did not have the opportunity to attend the funerals or recognize the deaths, a memorial service was held in the school to remember these students.

The following describes the service in detail, as an example for other schools to follow. Of course, each service will be different, but these are some of the things that can be done to help ease the pain of a death for students and teachers.

First Steps

To help plan the memorial service, the school contacted a local minister and funeral director. The minister assisted with the structure of the service and provided suitable readings. The funeral director suggested a 'short service,' beginning and ending with music, and he offered to provide flowers and memorial books for the families. Each family was invited to attend and asked to lend the school a favourite eight-by-ten photograph of their son or daughter. The pictures were placed at the front of the auditorium on a table decorated with the school colours. The flower arrangements, also in school colours, were placed behind the table. The service called for a favourite teacher to speak about the deceased students, followed by a student who would recite a poem or give a scripture reading. The music was chosen by friends of the students, including an original work performed by a band in which one of the students had played guitar. The music was taped so that it could be replayed. Attendance at the service was voluntary. It was held near the end of the school day to recognize the importance of the event. An announcement was made earlier in the week to determine the number of students who felt they wanted to attend. After the service, a reception was held for the families, staff, and close friends in the school library. At the end of the service the students signed the memorial books and looked at the pictures. The flowers were donated to a local retirement home.

Although it was difficult for the parents and families to attend, everyone felt comforted by the fact that the school had remembered their children and their accomplishments. The service also helped to link the school and the community. The service also provided an opportunity for all students to acknowledge their feelings and grief over the death of their friends. It was, indeed, a time of sharing. The service was also recorded, and each family received a copy of the tape, along with the memorial books.

In advance of the service the principal made the following announcement over the school's PA system: 'As most students are aware, this summer has been very tragic for the friends and families of three students who died in motor vehicle accidents. Because these deaths occurred during the summer, many students were unable to attend funeral services for David, Karyl-Ann, and Scott. The school will be holding a memorial service to remember these students on Tuesday, October 13, at 2:30 p.m., for those students who would like to attend.'

The following pages describe in detail the service itself, including the content of the printed programs and all readings chosen by students and teachers.

THE SERVICE

MEMORIAL SERVICE IN COMMEMORATION OF

DAVID
KARYL-ANN
SCOTT
Tuesday, October 13, 1990
2:30 p.m.

Readings
Calling Together

'The Road of Life'
a poem by Karyl-Ann

Selected Readings

'Joy and Sorrow'
by Kahlil Gibran
Wisdom 3; Verses 1 to 3
John 14: 106; 18: 19, 17

Sending Forth   'Do Not Stand at My Grave'
                                 (author unknown)

Students wishing a copy of any of the readings utilized in today's service are invited to request them from the Counselling Office.

Program

PRELUDE
'Teach Your Children'
'The Rose'
'Let It Be'
'Bridge Over Troubled Waters'
(Audience is requested to stand at the entrance of our guests.)

THE CALLING TOGETHER   *Mr. G. Baxter*

READINGS AND REMEMBRANCES
David   *Mrs. S. Blazier*
                                 Heather
Karyl-Ann   *Mr. G. Campbell*
                                 Kirsti
Scott   *Mrs. Welton*
                                 Michael

REFLECTIONS IN PRAYER
A moment of silence   *Rev. W. Robert Johnstone*
The Lord's Prayer   *(Christ Church United)*

SENDING FORTH   *Mrs. S. Blazier*

BENEDICTION   *Rev. W. Robert Johnstone*
(Audience is requested to stand at the exit of our guests.)

SIGNING OF MEMORIAL BOOKS   *Mr. G. Baxter*
'Stairway to Heaven'
'The End'
'Side by Side' (a composition performed by D.O.G.)

THE ROAD OF LIFE

As we travel along the road of life,
We may encounter many holes along its path
As we very well know, we do not walk this path alone,
but with people we meet, so called friends.
The paths of these people are not like yours, and the
people drift apart.
This is because the two do not have time to wait,
or the energy to walk faster.
The people that are left behind, and the people that carry
on become the past.
After this happens, you are never alone for long
and the new people come along and the road begins again.
No matter how long the friendship, you never forget,
And maybe, you will meet again.

— Karyl-Ann

WISDOM 3; VERSES 1 to 3

But the soul of the virtuous are in the hands of God,
no torment shall ever touch them.
In the eyes of the unwise, they did appear to die,
their going looked like a disaster, their leaving us, like
annihilation;
But they are in peace.

JOHN 14: 1–6, 18: 19, 27

Jesus said, 'Let not your hearts be troubled; believe in God,
believe also in me. In my Father's house are many rooms; if it
were not so, would I have told you that I go to prepare a place
for you? And when I go and prepare a place for you, I will come
again and will take you to myself, that where I am you may be
also. And you know the way where I am going.' Thomas said to

him, 'Lord we do not know where you are going; how can we know the way?' Jesus said to him, 'I am the way, and the truth, and the life; no one comes to the Father, but by me.'

'I will not leave you desolate; I will come to you. Yet a little while, and the world will see me no more, but you will see me; because I live you will live also.'

'Peace I leave with you; my peace I give to you; not as the world gives do I give to you. Let not your hearts be troubled, neither let them be afraid.'

DO NOT STAND AT MY GRAVE

Do not stand at my grave and weep.
I am not there,
I do not sleep.
Look for me on the fresh fallen snow,
And the many winds that blow.
I am the glistening stars at night.
I am the beautiful rays of the morning light.
Do not stand at my grave and cry.
I am not there.
I did not die!

— Author unknown

OTHER READINGS

JOY AND SORROW

Then a woman said, Speak to us of Joy and Sorrow.
And he answered:
And the Selfsame well from which your laughter rises was oftentimes filled
with your tears.

And how else can it be?

The deeper that sorrow carves into your being, the more joy you can contain.

Is not the cup that holds your wine the very cup that was burned in the potter's oven? And is not the lute that soothes your spirit, the very wood that was hollowed with knives? When you are joyous, look deep into your heart and you shall find it is only that which has given you sorrow that is giving you joy.

When you are sorrowful look again in your heart, and you shall see that in truth you are weeping for that which has been your delight.

Some of you say, 'Joy is greater than sorrow,' and others say, 'Nay, sorrow is the greater.'

But I say unto you, they are inseparable. Together they come, and when one sits alone with you at your board, remember that the other is asleep upon your bed.

Verily you are suspended like scales between your sorrow and your joy.

Only when you are empty are you at a standstill and balanced.

When the treasure-keeper lifts you to weigh his gold and his silver, needs must your joy or sorrow rise or fall.

— Kahlil Gibran

DEATH

Then Almitra spoke, saying, We would ask now of Death.

And he said:

You would know the secret of death.

But how shall you find it unless you seek it in the heart of life?

The owl whose night-bound eyes are blind unto the day cannot unveil the mystery of light. If you would indeed behold the spirit of death, open your heart wide unto the body of life. For life and death are one, even as the river and the sea are one.

In the depth of your hopes and desires lies your silent knowledge of the beyond;

And like seeds dreaming beneath the snow your heart dreams of spring.

Trust the dreams, for in them is hidden the gate to eternity.
Your fear of death is but the trembling of the shepherd when he
stands before the king whose hand is to be laid upon him in
honour.
Is the shepherd not joyful beneath his trembling, that he shall
wear the mark of the king?
Yet is he not more mindful of his trembling?

For what is it to die but to stand naked in the wind and to melt
into the sun?
And what is it to cease breathing, but to free the breath from its
restless tides, that it may rise and expand and seek God unen-
cumbered?

Only when you drink from the river of silence shall you indeed
sing.
And when you have reached the mountain top, then you shall
begin to climb.
And when the earth shall claim your limbs, then shall you truly
dance.

Epilogue

Yesterday

I find myself thinking about yesterday.

When we were together.
'Forever together,' we said.

When we would talk,
Or,
When we would just stare.

When we would dance,
Or,
When we would just watch others.

When we would sing,
Or,
When we would just listen.

When we would laugh,
Or,
When we would just smile.

When we would kiss,
Or,
When we would just hold each other.

Memories of yesterday,
Are all that remain.

When I sit by myself and think,
Or,
When I just cry.

— Cory

Appendix 1
Religious Beliefs and Funeral Practices

Canada is a multicultural country, and chances are adolescents in bereavement groups will have a variety of reactions to death, funerals, and religious rites, depending on the cultural and religious beliefs of their countries of origin. This appendix is intended to give leaders of adolescent bereavement groups a brief look at some of the beliefs and practices they are likely to encounter and will need to consider in order to understand what their group members are going through following a death.

First, however, it should be noted that past experience with bereavement groups has shown many common reactions among adolescents to the rituals surrounding death. Even when they do not have firm religious beliefs, most adolescents want to believe that the soul of a loved one is in some special place. For some, visiting the cemetery is very comforting; they like to visit daily, if they live nearby, in order to commune with the spirit of the loved one buried there. When they come away from such visits, they feel better able to cope. However, for others the cemetery is not a comforting place; these adolescents say they 'feel weird' at the thought of the body of their loved one being there, and often have nightmares after visiting the cemetery. As well, almost all adolescents seem to feel it is not right to have a 'so-called party' (a wake) after the funeral, especially when alcoholic beverages are involved. They do not understand how adults can be crying and sad at one moment and happily partying the next.

All adolescents have many questions – about funeral homes, cremation, what the rituals and beliefs are in a place of worship other than their own. They may want a few facts, or even detailed descriptions, but they need answers that are not frightening. Brief answers to some of these questions follow.

The Funeral Home

Most religious traditions provide a place where family and friends may meet and express condolences, and where funeral services are often held. The body is sometimes present, sometimes not. A book is signed and remembrances are shared. Adolescents need to know that one needn't say much, or stay long.

Cremation

Adolescents are curious about cremation. How is it done? What do ashes look like? What do you do with them?

In brief, cremation is the process of reducing the body to bone fragments by intense heat (approximately 1,000 degrees Celsius (1,830 degrees Fahrenheit) for two to three hours. The cremated remains, commonly referred to as ashes, are then removed from the cremation chamber. (They weigh, normally, between one and three kilograms – three to six pounds.) At this time the remains of the casket (latches, screws, etc.) are removed. The ashes are then processed into finer fragments and placed in a temporary container, then a permanent one if the family has made such arrangements. Depending on the policy of the crematorium, family members can sometimes be present for the cremation. Some families choose to bury the urn in the cemetery; others choose to take the urn home.

The practice, chosen by some, to keep the urn on a mantlepiece or shelf at home is almost guaranteed to make adolescents uneasy. Whatever the ultimate decision concerning disposal of ashes, all adolescents feel happier when ashes are scattered, buried, or otherwise entombed.

Funeral Rites

Protestant

With the exception of the Anglican church, which prefers that funerals be held in the church itself, most Protestant services can be held in the funeral home or other chapel, and – rarely – at the home of the deceased. Services include sacred music and/ or music favoured by the deceased or by the family, prayer, a reading of the obituary, scripture readings, a sermon or talk about the person's life, often by the priest or minister, but sometimes by a family member or friend. The service can be followed by a brief service at the gravesite or following cremation. Most services are followed by a tea or lunch at the church, chapel, funeral home, or sometimes at the family home, where mourners can meet and talk. Often, donations are made to a charity in memory of the deceased, or flowers are sent to the funeral or to the home. A commemorative stone or plaque is placed on the grave, usually within a year of the death.

Roman Catholic

Funeral observances in the Catholic church, as with Protestant services, may include a eulogy, scripture readings, sacred and secular music, and the gathering of family members and friends following the service. The central difference is the celebration of the Mass, offered for the repose of the soul of the deceased.

Though cremation is not forbidden, internment is preferred, in a Catholic cemetery consecrated by the church. Again, donations may be made to a charity in memory of the deceased, or flowers may be sent to the church or the family home. It is common in the Catholic church for mourners to arrange through the church office for a Mass to be said for the soul of the deceased, after which a Mass card acknowledging the Mass and the donor is sent to the family.

Eastern Orthodox

The Eastern Orthodox church forbids cremation. Families quite often arrange for their loved ones to be buried in the country where they were born. Some believers, particularly in the Mediterranean, still disinter the bones of the deceased after many years have passed, and store the remains in ossuaries. It is common to bury the dead in shrouds rather than in coffins, and in very deep graves. Family members wear black for one year of strict mourning, during which time all socializing is discouraged.

Hindu

The funeral is held in a funeral home, usually the day of the death, and is traditionally conducted by the first-born son. Mourners wear white; visitors, subdued colours. There is little outward mourning if the deceased is elderly, but a sense of tragedy is evident in mourners if the deceased is young. The family is expected to enter a period of mourning for thirteen days, depending on its caste. At the end of that time the family sponsors a feast for close friends and relatives. All bodies are cremated and the ashes usually returned to India to be scattered in the Ganges.

Baha'i

Baha'i law stipulates that a body may not be transported more than one hour's journey from the place of death to the place of internment. Embalming is not allowed and all bodies are buried, not cremated, though exceptions are sometimes made in cases of contagious disease. The funeral is handled by the local spiritual assembly. As there are no clergy, the service is conducted by the family. Each service is unique with one exception: the family must offer a specific Prayer for the Dead. After burial it is customary that the family invite friends to their home for a meal.

Confucian, Taoist, Buddhist

In all three traditions cremation is preferred, though burial is also accepted. Funeral services may vary depending on the country of origin of believers. Most services take place at the funeral home. It is appropriate to send flowers. Only one night of visitation is held. Shoes, traditionally removed in temple services, may be left on for the visitation or funeral. A table is set up to hold candles and incense, which burn until the body is moved to the cemetery or crematorium. Visitors often make a donation to the family. The funeral service is conducted by a monk, with prayers and chanting (visitors are not expected to participate). At the conclusion of the service, mourners come forward as a group and bow to the casket to show their final respects. Each visitor is given an envelope containing a coin for good luck and a candy to take away the bitter taste of death. After the service at the cemetery, family and close friends usually meet at a restaurant to share a meal together.

Sikh

Funeral services are held at a funeral home. In Canada the deceased is clothed in a new suit or sari and placed in a casket. The heads of all mourners must be covered. Passages from the Sikh holy book are read and prayers offered. Relatives and friends recite scriptural hymns; they are discouraged from crying. The body is transported to the crematorium, where another service is performed. Shoes must be removed, heads must be covered, and women and men are seated separately. A meal is shared together at the temple. Sending flowers and cards is appropriate and appreciated.

Islamic

Cremation is strictly forbidden. The deceased must be interred within twenty-four hours of death. Before burial the body is washed by the family and placed in a shroud. The funeral service is usually held in a mosque, but may be held in a funeral chapel or at the cemetery, provided it is away from the grave site. While accompanying a funeral, silence is observed. Before the body is lowered into the grave, it is turned slightly so that it rests on its right side and the grave faces Mecca. All those present participate by adding at least three handfuls of earth to the grave. Mourners wail loudly, place flowers on the grave. Forty days of mourning are observed.

Judaic

With the exception of Reform and Liberal synagogues, cremation is forbidden, since resurrection is a cardinal dogma and destruction of the body by cremation is a denial of resurrection.

Upon hearing of a death, a Jew recites, 'Blessed be the true judge,' therefore performing the rite of Kerih, that is, making a slight tear in his clothing as a sign of mourning. Jewish tradition frowns on embalming unless required by law. It is seen as a violation of the sanctity of the body.

It is also customary as a sign of grief to cover up or put away all mirrors or other decorative objects. A large candle is lit and renewed for thirty days, except on the Sabbath. Since embalming is forbidden, especially for Orthodox Jews, the funeral usually takes place within twenty-four hours with a closed casket and immediate burial. The deceased is bathed and ritually cleansed (Taharah), then placed in a simple white shroud (Tachrichin), all burial tasks being performed by a volunteer society of pious Jews. *No visitation is permitted before the funeral service.* The service may consist of psalms, a eulogy, and the memorial prayer. A eulogy is generally delivered only for distinguished men or scholars. Pious Jews arrange to have a little sack of Palestinian soil in the caskets, and their bodies are placed in the ground, facing Zion.

The surviving members of the immediate family then sit Shivah, seven days of mourning during which they do not leave the house, remaining at home for visitors to come and console them. The children of the deceased recite prayers three times a day for eleven months, adding the Kaddish, a special prayer in honour of the dead. Every year the anniversary of the death is observed at home and in the synagogue by the lighting of the memorial lamp for twenty-four hours. At the end of the first year, a memorial stone is set up in the cemetery.

The Orthodox Jewish funeral is held in the synagogue or funeral home. It is customary not to send flowers to the funeral home. Friends and relatives may call at the residence. A period of mourning usually follows the burial.

The Reform service is similar to the Protestant service. Flowers are sent, visitation is held, and the funeral is conducted at the temple or funeral home. Following the burial a memorial service at the residence is also part of the Reform ritual.

Jewish tradition understands that the healing process after a loss is a slow, organic one and there are a series of rituals to be observed (the funeral home provides a calendar):

- – Shiva: Seven days of mourning are observed.
- – Shloshim: Thirty days after the death, a candle is lit.
- – Kaddish: Special prayers are said.
- – Yahrzelt: One year after the death, a candle is lit the night before, to gather the family together.

Memorial services take place in the synagogue four times a year – at Yom Kippur, Pesach, Shavuot, and Succot – creating a time to honour and remember those who have died.

Zoroastrian

Zoroastrians are known for their veneration of Fire, Water, and Earth, which they consider sacred. Thus, they have a unique burial practice in their country of origin: modern-day Iran. They build high towers of silence in which they leave their dead to vultures and birds of prey. In Canada the deceased is always cremated and the urn goes to the cemetery, but is not buried. A service is held in the funeral home. Flowers are sent in remembrance. Once the priest has blessed the body, it then cannot be touched. After the service, friends and relatives go to the family home for a meal. There can be no television, radio, etc. during the week of mourning. The priest visits the home, prayers are regularly said, and there is a special ceremony to commemorate the first anniversary of the death.

Appendix 2
Research with Bereaved Teenagers

A summary of a 1984 research paper by Ross E. Gray is included here to illustrate the need for bereavement groups, a need that is too often overlooked.[1]

This paper will focus on selected aspects of a larger research study. In particular, the perceptions of bereaved teenagers about who was helpful to them in dealing with their loss will be addressed. This information will then be related to the roles of school counsellors and other school staff. As well, the perceptions of those teenagers who were involved in peer support groups will be presented and discussed.

A Brief Description of the Study

Fifty persons participated in this study, all of whom have lost a parent through death during adolescence, and within the last five years. A semi-structured interview was employed in which participants were asked to rate the helpfulness of various people in dealing with their loss. They were also asked to describe the ways in which others were helpful. All but a few of the participants were students within the Peel Board of Education at the time of the interview. Half of them had been involved in a peer support group for bereaved teenagers at their school, while the

---

1 Paper toward a doctoral degree, Ontario Institute for Studies in Education, 1984.

remainder of the participants had not belonged to a support group. Support group participants attended either Lorne Park, Cawthra Park or Streetsville Secondary School, and the rest of the Peel Board participants attended one of a variety of other schools within the system.

Perception of the Helpfulness of Others

There was a great deal of variation amongst participants as to how helpful family members were perceived as being in dealing with their loss. For example, 34% of teenagers reported that their surviving parent was 'very helpful,' while 30% rated the parent as 'not at all helpful.' Often it seemed to be difficult for family members to share with, and support each other, either because of absorption with their own grief or because of a perceived need to protect others from distress. Some teenagers reported wishing they had had more support than was offered. One of the possible implications of these findings is that counsellors may sometimes be able to play a role in facilitating family relations following a loss. One aspect of such a potential role might be to encourage parent-teenager communication around the mutual task of mourning.

A second aspect might be to discuss with teenagers some of the inevitable difficulties that arise within a family as a result of losing one of its members. For example, several participants in this study commented that it had been helpful to talk with a counsellor about problems they were having with the surviving parent, or with a new step-parent.

Bereaved teenagers in this study most often reported that the 'most helpful person' in dealing with their loss was a peer. This was true for teenagers with and without support group involvement. Despite this finding, however, many participants reported that only one or two friends had been helpful, or that just peers in the support group had been helpful. Too frequently, the larger network of peers seemed to withdraw from the bereaved person, leaving them feeling socially isolated and abnormal. Most teenagers said that they did not want to be treated in a special way by their peers and that they wanted to be included in activities as usual. This did not seem to be entirely true for close friends, who were often seen as people who could be confided in or who could provide other kinds of emotionally sustaining support.

How might high school students learn more about how they could be helpful when a peer suffers a loss? One strategy would be to use a global educational approach and try to find a way for such information to be included in the curriculum. Although perhaps not ideal, this would be a large task and success may not be likely in the foreseeable future. Another, more creative, strategy for educating peers might be to approach the friends of a bereaved teenager and discuss some of the ways that they could potentially be helpful. The peer support group is another model intended to make it more likely that peers will be experienced and helpful, and there is some evidence that this does occur. For example, support group participants in this study were much more likely to report that they had felt understood by peers following their loss than did other bereaved teenagers. Another interesting finding was that support group participants less often reported that peers had been helpful by distracting them from the pain of their loss. Perhaps this shows that the kinds of support available through groups aided teenagers to overcome the urge to flee the pain of mourning.

Participants in the study reported that teachers were often unhelpful (42%) or were only helpful in minimal ways. Although it could be expected that teachers would not play a major role in the support of bereaved teenagers, there were ways of being helpful that were often neglected. Simple statements of being sorry, or offers of being willing to talk, were often experienced as helpful – as long as they were expressed in private. Helpfulness was frequently experienced when a teacher was willing to adjust his or her expectations to allow for the distress of the bereaved student. Such adjustments included spending extra time with a student on academic assignments, rescheduling exams and extending due dates.

Some teachers were able to provide support of a more emotionally sustaining style. This tended to occur when the teacher had been close to the student prior to the loss, or when the teacher was able to talk about his or her own experience(s) of loss with the student.

Many participants described ways in which teachers were not helpful to them. It was generally agreed, for example, that teachers who told students to buckle down and focus on their schoolwork were not helpful. It is unrealistic to expect students who have recently suffered a loss to keep their academic work up to pre-loss standards. It was also considered unhelpful if teachers drew attention to the student's loss in front of other students. This only served to embarrass them. A few students reported dealing with teachers who were openly hostile to them following their loss. In such unfortunate cases, the teacher's own obvious inability to handle loss and suffering caused great difficulties for students. There is, then, a potential role for counsellors in informing teachers about how they can be helpful and in advocating on behalf of students who are not being treated in an appropriately sensitive manner.

The perceived helpfulness of school counsellors and school nurses was dramatically higher for teenagers who had been in a support group than for those who had not. This does not necessarily mean that one needs to start a peer support group in order to be helpful. It does mean, however, that without a formal intervention program like the peer support group, some difficulties may arise which make helpfulness less likely. Firstly, there may be more problems in relation to the identification of bereaved persons in the school. At a number of schools contacted for this study, counsellors were unable to identify any students who had lost a parent. This improbable situation would suggest that the school's system of detecting and transmitting such important information was inadequate. Counsellors cannot be of assistance if they don't know about a loss. Another problem that can develop is that counsellors may tend to focus exclusively on academic problems. This may sometimes occur if a student comes to the counsellor's attention due to a sudden drop in grades. Several teenagers expressed resentment about counsellors who they felt were only worried about their marks and not about them. Although it can be useful to give assistance around academic issues, there are other ways of reaching out that may also be useful. All persons engaged in the mourning process have to deal with difficult, painful emotions, and it may be helpful for them to have some space in which these can be allowed and accepted as normal. Counsellors may be able to provide this space for some teenagers.

It is often difficult to approach bereaved teenagers about their loss. They may be reluctant to talk about it and/or they may feel embarrassed that they are now seen as different and in need of help.

Too often, open-ended invitations to bereaved teenagers to come and talk if they want were not accepted due to the teenagers' feelings of awkwardness. It would seem more appropriate to find a way of regularly checking in with a student to ask how things are going, make some gentle probes and allow the student a chance to express himself or herself. If a student does not want to talk about the loss, that is fine, but at least he or she may feel cared for.

With such a strategy, it would, of course, be important to avoid the student's coming to feel stigmatized by his or her work with a counsellor. It may be necessary to arrange meetings in ways that will not cause peers to think that the bereaved student 'needs' help. As well, in any exchanges of information, it is essential that the normality of the difficult aspects of mourning be continually stressed. It is extremely helpful for students to know that what they are experiencing is in no way pathological.

Often there is a tendency for helping professionals to try to find ways to make everything better. Certainly it is important that we do what we can to relieve unnecessary suffering, but one of the most fundamental aspects of dealing with a bereaved person is the need to recognize that the person needs to feel pain if he or she is going to later be able to reinvest in life in a healthy way. It will be helpful if a counsellor is able to accept a student's suffering and let him or her know that it is both acceptable and normal.

Perceptions of the Peer Support Program

Those teenagers who had participated in a peer support group were asked some specific questions regarding their experience. This information may be useful to individuals who are currently leading such groups or who are considering doing so in the future.

All of the bereaved teenagers were approached about their possible participation in a support group on an individual basis, and this was perceived as being both appropriate and sensitively handled. When teenagers were seen for this initial interview, they were usually told that the group was for support and not for therapy. Approximately two-thirds of the group remembered being given this information and slightly less than half felt that it was important information to have. This would seem to suggest that most teenagers may not make meaningful discriminations between these two different intervention models and that such reassurances may be less necessary than counsellors have sometimes believed them to be.

Group meetings were held at different times across the three schools in which interviews were conducted. The large majority of persons, regardless of which school they attended, felt that their group was held at the 'best possible time.' This unilateral response may indicate that there is actually no best time for having group meetings and that teenagers will tend to use whatever opportunity they have to engage in the work of mourning. Although several participants expressed a wish that group meetings be held outside of regular school hours, by far the majority liked having the meetings during school hours.

The number of weeks over which support groups met varied by school, with one school averaging seven to nine weeks, and the others averaging ten to twelve weeks. Twenty-five per cent of participants felt that the groups should have been longer, 17% felt they should have been shorter, and the rest were satisfied with the length of their group. One possible solution to such different needs would be to give students an option of continuing for three or four sessions after the first seven or eight meetings. This would allow students who felt they needed more time to have it and students who felt finished to drop out in an acceptable manner. In relation to this issue of the time frame over which groups should be run, it is interesting to note that 40% of the teenagers interviewed said they would have liked some kind of structured ongoing support after the group ended. Although students were invariably told to drop in and talk with group leaders if they wanted, this kind of contact was too difficult for some teenagers to initiate. It may, therefore, be more useful to formally structure ongoing contacts with students after the group ends – unless they prefer not to.

Group participants were asked about who should be allowed to belong to bereavement support groups. Most students felt that if someone close to an individual had died, then they should be allowed to participate in a group. A minority of students felt that group membership should be limited to those who had lost an immediate family member. An interesting finding is that over 90% of participants felt that it would be inappropriate to *include students in the group who had lost a parent through divorce* rather than through death.

All group participants said that they felt cared for and respected by group leaders. This should provide leaders with a well-justified measure of satisfaction about the way they are relating to students. Approximately two-thirds of the teenagers stated that participation in a bereavement support group made a positive difference to the way they are now. Some others felt that although the group was interesting and/or helpful, it did not make a major difference to their lives.

Former group members were asked to recommend possible way of improving support group functioning. Although many participants had no recommendations, some did, and these are as follows:

1. A limit should be put on the number of persons to be included in a group. Several teenagers mentioned that their group had been too large for everyone to get a chance to express themselves adequately. Estimates of the ideal group size ranged from five to eight.
2. Participants should be free to attend or not attend the group. Several students felt that too much pressure had been put on them to attend. This is a difficult issue, as a certain amount of commitment is needed from students if the group is to be effective. Certainly, this should be stressed in the first sessions of the group, but beyond that, it may be counterproductive to pursue students who are not attending.
3. Parents should receive more information about the group. It is, of course, important that students' rights for privacy be

maintained, but there would appear to be a good case to be made for parents receiving more information about the general purpose and functioning of the group than they often do. Several participants wondered if a separate parents' group might be possible. One person thought that it would be a good idea to have the group make a presentation to the parents towards the end of the group's sessions. These or other strategies might be employed to make a better link between the group and the parents of bereaved teenagers.

4. Provide a few more structured activities. Although most participants seemed satisfied with the level of structure in the group, several felt that more activities might make it less likely that one or two people would monopolize the group's time.

At this point, I would like to add some personal thoughts about the peer support group program in the Peel Board. Perhaps it is appropriate to begin with some possible difficulties.

Although there is a good case to be made for the value of bereavement support groups in the school, it should always be remembered that, as with any intervention model, there are limits to its usefulness. It is, for example, important to remember that the effects of loss can run very deep and that these effects may not always be ameliorated by this or any formal intervention. One relevant finding from the present study is that bereaved teenagers, regardless of whether or not they participated in a peer support group, scored higher on an objective depression inventory than has been reported elsewhere with non-bereaved teenagers. The finding that bereavement may have an ongoing effect despite intervention is consistent with the evidence available from other studies. When we recognize the limitations of intervention strategies, we may have more compassion for ourselves when everything doesn't go the way we had hoped. As well, such a recognition may sensitize us to the frequent need to follow-up when formal interventions come to an end.

Another issue to consider is that of whether the support group model is necessarily the best model for all situations and all teenagers. Several of the teenagers I talked with said that they preferred to talk with their counsellor one to one rather than to

discuss things in the group. For some, the more traditional coun-
sellor-student interaction may be the appropriate one. An alternative model which would focus on facilitating the support within
the teenager's already existing social network may also be a valid
alternative. Indeed, there is a danger that the support group
may come to replace this natural network in the short term
dealing with loss, and this should be avoided at all costs. Ideally,
the combination of support group and facilitating of support
from an existing network could be very effective. The point,
then, is that the support group model is one of a number of
models that can be helpful to bereaved teenagers.

None of the above-mentioned will be helpful if counsellors
who are using them are not relatively comfortable with issues
related to loss and death. This common sense observation should
lead us to recognize that peer support groups will only be appropriate where there are school staff who are willing and able to
tolerate a great deal of suffering. An indiscriminate spread of
peer support groups in the school system could do more harm
than good.

Other limitations which can occur in relation to peer support
groups are related to the needs for adequate planning and for
communication between group leaders. In the course of my research, I learned that most guidance counsellors have very heavy
working schedules. Unfortunately, this may sometimes lead to
cutting corners in relation to the functioning of groups. It seems
to me to be crucially important that group leaders meet between
sessions. Therefore, this should be a top priority use of time.
Another related issue has to do with potential value for counsellors of receiving feedback about their interactions with, and understanding of, bereaved students. It is common for all of us to
develop blind spots in our interactions with others, or to have
difficulties in dealing with specific kinds of problems that arise.
Meetings between leaders of peer support groups in the different schools might allow for mutually beneficial learning experiences. As well, regular consultations between group leaders and
an outside resource person might be valuable.

Now that I have presented some of my concerns about support groups, I would like to state that I believe these groups to

be very useful. Certainly the testimonies of the teenagers interviewed have convinced me that many have benefited enormously. I experienced the leaders of these support groups to be, without exception, warm and caring human beings. The Peel Board of Education is a leader in Canada in dealing with bereaved teenagers, largely because of the creative interest and compassion-in-action of such front line staff.

Conclusion

There continue to be ways in which we can all improve our caring for bereaved teenagers – in schools that have peer support groups, in schools that do not, and in the wider community. Learning to actively care for those who are suffering is not one of those tasks for which there would seem to be an ultimate endpoint or an easy solution. It is an inherently difficult task and yet one which is extremely worthy of our continued attention and effort.

Appendix 3
Articles

The following articles were written after Lorne Park Secondary School bereavement group members were interviewed concerning their experience with the groups. (Bereaved Families of Ontario did not offer such groups for adolescents at the time, and the articles encouraged the young people to approach their own schools for help.) The articles also illustrate the complexity of bereavement in today's society, and will interest anyone interested in conducting adolescent bereavement groups.

The Early Death of a Parent
Aftermath of the Loss Can Follow a Child Right through Life

by Leslie Scrivener, *Toronto Star,* 17 April 1981

She thought she had stored the memories of her mother's death away forever. But after half a century, there they were, disturbing and confusing her at age 61.

When she was 11, she was awakened in the middle of the night and told her mother was dead. Later, at the funeral, she was told to wait in the car while her relatives attended the burial service. She resented that she hadn't been allowed to participate and mourn with her family. A year later, her father left her in the care of her grandmother.

Her relatives had good intentions which, in the long run, may have proven harmful. When her mother died, her grandmother and aunt told her that God took her mother because she was so good. 'Can you imagine what a burden that was on a little girl? She's too good to live and I'm left here. I had to be twice as good to make up for her not being here.'

This woman, an executive secretary, is still working out the meaning of those memories, which surfaced after the death of her husband three years ago. When she started seeing a counsellor recently for what she thought to be the pre-retirement blues, the memories of past losses cascaded out. Why was she always struggling to be so independent? Was it connected with the loss of her parents? Why should these memories trouble her now, after so many years.

She's still seeking the answers.

Effects Can Last

The effects of a parent's death during childhood or adolescence can last through adulthood. Helping a child cope with the death of a parent, to avoid problems in later life, is one of the most puzzling issues in psychology, says Stephen Fleming, a professor of psychology at York University and consultant to the hospice program at the York-Finch Hospital.

If the experiences concerning a parent's death have been unpleasant or repressed – as in the case of the 61-year-old woman above – a child may grow into a highly distrustful adult, supersensitive to any loss (a broken friendship, a job, moving to a new neighbourhood) and, according to some studies, suffer more intense depressions than most other people. He or she may also be reluctant to start adult relationships, suspecting at every turn that he'll be hurt again. However, these experiences need not occur if the surviving parent or guardian shows love and is close to the child during the difficult times.

In fact, current research shows that it is the sense of loss, not just the fact of death, that affects children most profoundly, says professor Richard Lonetto of the University of Guelph, author of the book *Children's Conceptions of Death*.

Death itself does cause psychological problems, says Fleming of York University, but there is a correlation between insensitive handling of death and problems in adulthood.

Still Surprised

A 30-year-old Toronto woman who lost both her parents before she was 13 admits she is still surprised at the bitterness that surfaces during sessions with her psychiatrist. Her parents' names were never mentioned after their death because her relatives thought she would be too upset.

'You feel cynical now,' says the woman. 'The child who loses her parents at a young age becomes cynical at a young age. You never forgive them because you've been forced into maturity at an early age and it's eternal punishment.'

Feelings of rejection and guilt, that somehow the child was responsible for the death, are among the most common reactions. A 28-year-old working mother, whose father left home and whose mother committed suicide when the woman was ten, is still tormented by those feelings as well as by a bitterness. 'I was very angry with her and still am,' she says. 'People with moms and dads have a cushion to fall on if their marriage falls apart, or whatever ... when I was pregnant I thought about my mother a lot. I wished she had had the strength to stay around. Now I'm always thinking life is going to turn around and slap me in my face, that something might happen to my little boy. We are happy, but I always think this happiness isn't going to last.'

The death of a mother may be more traumatic than the death of a father, says Lonetto, because a child is used to seeing his father go away and come back while his mother may be a constant presence in his life. However, the sudden death of a parent of either sex is likely to have a greater long-term effect on a child than death following a lengthy illness, because no one has had time to prepare for the loss, he says.

It may be an unreliable cliché to say that boys who lose their mothers grow into men who never trust or who deliberately try to hurt women, says Fleming. 'It's too obvious and there's no conclusive data to support it,' he says.

Child Angry

Some of the problems in failing to help children cope with death may spring from adults' attempts to protect children from death and grieving. 'One woman asked a friend to take her child to the zoo while the rest of the family was grieving at her husband's funeral,' says Joy Rogers, a mental health consultant at the Clarke Institute of Psychiatry and lecturer at the University of Toronto. 'The child was seeing lions and tigers, having a special occasion, while this was going on. When the child found out, she was very angry. No one had even asked her what she wanted.'

While most death experiences can be handled in the home by understanding friends and relatives – 'we don't need to professionalize bereavement,' says Rogers – sometimes the surviving parent is incapacitated by grief. 'Children have almost a double problem,' she says. 'When one parent dies, it's almost like losing two parents, one to grief, and it's hard to be a parent when you're paralyzed by your own sorrow.'

However, a recent join effort by school nurses, counsellors and a social worker has resulted in two successful school groups for grieving students. The groups may work because children are in a familiar setting among people they feel comfortable with.

Angry Kids

Organized at Lorne Park and Cawthra secondary schools in Mississauga, Ontario, the projects help children who have suffered physical and mental distress following a death in the family. They have been troubled by everything from ulcers to failing grades or an incommunicative parent.

'Kids have talked about being angry, unprepared and bitter because they weren't told the whole truth,' says social worker Laurie Bennett, from the Mississauga Hospital. Some students were not told their parent was dying and felt guilty because they didn't go to the hospital. Her advice to parents to help children cope:

- Tell kids the truth no matter what age they are. If a father has died, don't say he's going away. The child then may become terrified if his mother says she's going away, fearing she may never come back either.
- Share your sorrow with your children. A grieving parent should show tears, that it's okay to feel sad.

- Include children, especially older ones, in bereavement from the beginning. Ask younger children if they want to be involved and tell them what to expect. It may be helpful to ask a family friend to look after a child in case the parent breaks down during the ceremony. The child should be allowed to leave the ceremony when he wants.

Grieving Students Find Solace at School

by Dennis Hanagan, *Toronto Star,* 24 January 1984.

It was five months after the death of her younger sister that Jill Williams was suddenly overwhelmed by the loss. The girl, suffering from bone cancer, died one day short of her 13th birthday.

'It registered on me one day during a test (at school). I started crying and left the class ... we were very close,' says Williams, a 16-year-old student at Lorne Park Secondary School (in Mississauga, Ontario). She occupied much of her spare time afterward with long walks and she cringed at the thought of Christmas approaching; it used to be a time she and her sister would bake cookies together.

Intense Grief

But despite her intense grief, she was able to find some solace through a relatively new program at her school known as the Bereavement Support Group for students. The program gives students who have lost a relative or close friend a chance to discuss with one another problems and feelings about the death.

It started in 1979 after student counsellors and the school nurse determined that for many of the students who were seeing them, grief was the root of their troubles. Sorrow surfaced in the form of headaches or stomachaches. Some students missed classes, didn't complete assignments or plunged into depression. It was decided that a bereavement support group might be an answer for these young people, says Grant Baxter, head of student counselling services at Lorne Park.

Before the program, students were counselled individually, but as more students came, group sessions became a more efficient way to help. Laurie Bennett, who works with terminally ill patients and their families at Mississauga Hospital , helped launch the program. She instructed Baxter and school nurse, Wendy Stuart, for 20 hours in topics such as normal and abnormal grief, spiritual aspects of death and matters concerning funerals.

The group, averaging ten students at a time, meets for an hour a week during the school day in an informal setting in Stuart's office where they can sit on floor cushions and drink pop or smoke. No ringing telephones are allowed to interrupt the sometimes crucial discussions. Groups last about three months.

For Williams, who found her regular friends ill at ease around her, it was a chance to see how other young people reacted to death. 'I found out I was normal,' she says.

Teenagers have a difficult time coping with death, Bennett says. She has observed teens around dying people, 'and it wasn't difficult to see they were having a hard time.' Some run from the hospital room, she says.

Negative Effect

Adults tend to hide their grief and that can have a negative effect on the young person, who then isn't sure what his reaction should be. 'He has no role model ... when (death) hits he has feelings and no way of knowing that's normal, and that normal grief is healthy,' she says. And despite good intentions, adults generally create a condition in which young people are hit extra hard by death. A teen may be told a parent is entering hospital, but no mention is made the parent won't come out, thus leaving the teen unprepared for the inevitable.

'We try to protect them and end up betraying them,' Bennett says. A prepared teen might be more understanding toward a dying person, more helpful, and that could ease the eventual impact of death.

Breaks Tension

Bennett says students need a few months, some a few years, to accept a death. In the group, they're reminded it's all right to cry. Sometimes laughter breaks the tension when a member recalls a humorous incident with the deceased.

Some students think they see or hear the deceased and wonder whether they're going crazy, but hallucinating is normal, Bennett says. For many, there's an abrupt change in their outlook on life. 'They feel different inside and they are different in a sense,' Bennett says. 'It's almost the end of their childhood.' The oldest son may have to take the role of the lost father; the daughter takes the place of the mother. They suddenly find themselves leaned on psychologically by other family members. 'The family unit has to be restructured,' Bennett says. 'Often people don't know how to relate to each other any more.'

Other Peel secondary schools have adopted the bereavement program: Applewood, Cawthra Park and Centennial. This past spring, the Canadian Broadcasting Corporation aired a movie it made of a film being produced to tell Peel teachers about the program. Inquiries were received from parents, children, teachers and counsellors. Some came from across the country. Some students even transfer from one school to another specifically to attend the groups.

In Peel, there are about a dozen counsellors qualified to lead the groups. Bennett says there are no plans to incorporate the program into elementary schools.

Andy Thomas was just turning 12 in the spring of 1978 when his father, a former school teacher, died in an accident on his dairy farm near New Liskeard in northern Ontario. He was opening an oil drum with a torch when it exploded, leaving him with third-degree burns to 95 percent of his body. Seeing the blackened figure of his father seeking relief under a shower, Andy became hysterical. He ran.

'I wish the group was there right after the accident,' says Andy, the oldest of four boys. The fact he communicated well with his mother provided some comfort. Later, in the group, he found more ears and hearts ready to listen. He was reassured there was nothing he could have done to help his father.

Sometimes teachers inadvertently cause problems. Some don't realize grief lasts a long time and think the student should 'pull up his socks.'

Stuart, who along with Baxter will see students on a one-to-one basis even after the group has ended, sees students drawing strength from the group. A depressed student may see another group member at school and figure that, if he can tough it out, 'then so can I,' Stuart explains.

Appendix 4
Community Resources

- Funeral homes: Often have educational facilities, information, and support for the bereaved. Some offer groups or will give referrals for additional help. Some have grief counsellors who will contact families after a death, and are available for private counselling sessions (though they don't often have extensive counselling degrees).
- Community health nurses: Listings are in the telephone book under public health. Most schools also have a community health nurse who will visit at least once a week.
- Churches, temples, and synagogues: Some offer groups to help the bereaved. More and more clergy are receiving education about grief and will counsel one-on-one.
- Social services: Social workers are trained to help bereaved families (usually at no cost).
- Bereaved Families of Ontario: Groups are available for adults, adolescents, and children; also individual counselling; referrals; support from others who have suffered as well; and self-help.
- Compassionate Friends: The organization offers self-help, support during bereavement.
- Hospices: Help for the dying, no-cost support for families with long-term illnesses, and usually bereavement support.
- Hospital social work departments: Look to the hospital that looked after the person who died; also the hospital's social work department.
- Distress centres: Information is in the telephone book (usually on the front page); centres give anonymous phone sup-

port from trained volunteers who give good information; available twenty-four hours a day.
- Suicide survivor support programs: Large cities (Toronto) have offered this type of specialized support, both individual and group (immediate). Listing is in the telephone book.
- Mental health clinics: All hospitals have separate clinics.
- Family physicians: Your physician knows your history and can refer you for some ongoing help.
- Private grief counsellors: Most have excellent training; try to get a referral from someone who knows their credentials; some are covered by public and private health plans. Listing in telephone book under Psychologists.

Selected Bibliography

General

Adams, David W., and Eleanor J. Deveau, eds. *Factors Influencing Children and Adolescents' Perceptions and Attitudes toward Death.* Vol. 1, *Beyond the Innocence of Childhood.* Amityville, N.Y.: Baywood, 1995. (Chapters by Deveau, Wass, and Fulton)

– *Helping Children and Adolescents Cope with Life-Threatening Illness and Dying.* Vol. 2, *Beyond the Innocence of Childhood.* Amityville, N.Y.: Baywood, 1995. (Chapters by Leenars and Wencstern; also Auden)

– *Helping Children and Adolescents Cope with Death and Bereavement.* Vol. 3, *Beyond the Innocence of Childhood.* Amityville, N.Y.: Baywood, 1995. (Chapters by Rando, Attig, Anderson and Miller, Wolfe and Senta, and Johnson)

Buchman, Robert. *I Don't Know What to Say: How to Help and Support Someone Who Is Dying.* Toronto: Key Porter, 1988.

Callwood, June. *Twelve Weeks in Spring.* Toronto: Lester & Orpen Dennys, 1986.

Corelli, Ray. 'Killing the Pain.' *Maclean's.* 29 January 1996.

Corr, Charles A., and D.E. Balk, eds. *Handbook of Adolescent Death and Bereavement.* New York: Springer, 1996. (Chapters by Balk and Corr, Jurich and Collins, Fleming and Balmer, Hogan and de Santis, and Stevenson and Stevenson)

Corr, Charles A., and D. Corr, eds. *Helping Children Cope with Death and Bereavement.* 2d ed. New York: Springer, 1995.

Corr, Charles A., and Joan McNeil, *Adolescence and Death.* New York: Springer, 1986.

Corr, Charles A., and H. Wass, eds. *Helping Children Cope with Death: Guidelines and Resources.* 2d ed. New York: Hemisphere, 1984.

Corr, Charles H., I. Nabe, and D. Corr, eds. *Death and Dying/Life and Living.* Belmont, Calif.: Brooks Cole, 1994.

Doka, Kenneth J., ed. *Children Mourning Children.* Bristol, Pa.: Taylor & Francis, 1995.

Fitzgerald, Helen. *The Mourning Handbook.* New York: Simon & Schuster, 1991.

Furman, Erana. *A Child's Parent Dies: Studies in Childhood Bereavement.* New Haven: Yale University Press, 1974.

Gravelle, Karen, and Charles Hoskins. *Teenagers Face to Face with Bereavement.* Englewood, N.J.: Simon & Schuster, 1989.

Grollman, Earl A. *Explaining Death to Children.* Boston: Beacon Press, 1968.

– *Talking about Death: A Dialogue between Parent and Child.* Boston: Beacon Press, 1976.

– *Living When a Loved One Has Died.* Boston: Beacon Press, 1977.

– *Straight Talk about Death for Teenagers.* Boston: Beacon Press, 1993.

Klass, D., S. Nickman, and P. Silverman, eds. *Continuing Bonds: New Understandings of Grief.* New York: Taylor & Francis, 1996.

Krementz, Jill. *How It Feels When a Parent Dies.* 2d ed. New York: Knopf, 1988.

Kübler-Ross, Elisabeth. *On Death and Dying.* New York: Macmillan, 1969.

– *To Live Until We Say Goodbye.* New York: Prentice Hall, 1978.

– *Questions and Answers on Death and Dying.* New York: Collier, 1993.

Kübler-Ross, Elisabeth, ed. *Death: The Final Stages of Growth.* New York: Prentice Hall, 1975.

Kushner, Harold S. *When Bad Things Happen to Good People.* New York: Schocken Books, 1981.

Leick, W., and M. Davidson-Weilson. *Healing Pain: Attachment, Loss and Grief Therapy.* New York: Routledge, Chapman & Hall, 1991.

Locke, Shirley. *Coping with Loss: A Guide for Caregivers.* Springfield, Ill.: Charles C. Thomas, 1994.

Morgan, J.C. *The Dying and the Bereaved Teenager.* Philadelphia: Charles Press, 1990.

Multifaith Information Manual. Toronto: Ontario Multifaith Council on Spiritual and Religious Care, 1995.

O'Toole, D. *Facing Change: Coming Together and Falling Apart in the Teen Years.* Burnsville, N.C.: Rainbow Connection, 1996.

Rando, T.A. *Grief, Dying and Death: Clinical Interventions for Caregivers.* Champaign, Ill.: Research Press, 1981.

Ryan, Cornelius, and Kathryn Morgan Ryan. *A Private Battle.* New York: Simon & Schuster, 1979.

Schneiderman, Gerald. *Coping with Death in the Family.* Toronto, Chima, 1979.

Shneidman, E. *Death: Current Perspectives.* 3d ed. Palo Alto, Calif.: Mayfield, 1984.

Staudacher, Carol. *Men and Grief.* Oakland, Calif.: New Harbinger, 1991.

Waxler-Morrison, Nancy, Joan M. Anderson and Elizabeth Richardson, eds. *Cross-cultural Caring.* Vancouver: University of British Columbia Press, 1990.

Wolfelt, Alan. *Helping Children Cope with Grief.* Muncie, Ind.: Accelerated Development, U.S., 1990.

Worden, James William. *Grief Counseling and Grief Therapy: A Handbook for the Mental Health Practitioner.* 2d ed. New York: Springer, 1991.

Wylie, Betty Jane. *Beginnings: A Book for Widows.* Toronto: McClelland & Stewart, 1977.

Suicide

Kuklin, S. *After a Suicide: Young People Speak Up.* New York: G.P. Putnam's Sons, 1994.

Leenaars, A., and S. Wenckstern. *Suicide Prevention in Schools.* New York: Hemisphere, 1991.

Marcus, Eric. *Why Suicide?* New York: HarperCollins, 1996.

Schleifer, Jay. *Everything You Need to Know about Teen Suicide.* 2d. ed. New York: Rosen Publishing Group, 1997.

Suicide Prevention Handbook. Hamilton: Board of Education for the City of Hamilton, 1987.

Wrobleski, Adina. *Suicide – Why?* Minneapolis: Afterworks, 1989.

– *Suicide Survivors.* Minneapolis: Afterworks, 1991.

Fiction

Blume, Judy. *Tiger Eyes.* Scarsdale, N.Y.: Bradbury Press, 1981.

Guest, Judith. *Ordinary People.* New York: Viking, 1976.

Klein, Norma. *Sunshine.* Translated by Roegsak Pancharoen. Bangkok: Bamrungsan, 1981.

Lowry, Lois. *A Summer to Die.* London, Ont.: Althouse Press, 1986.
Segal, Erich. *Love Story.* New York: Harper & Row, 1978.
Smith, Robert Kimmel. *Jane's House.* New York: Morrow, 1982.
Strasser, Todd. *Friends Till the End.* New York: Delacorte Press, 1981.
Wright, L.R. *The Favorite.* Toronto: Doubleday, 1982.